D1527188

CHRISTIANITY WITHOUT BELIEFS

MARSHALL DAVIS

Copyright © 2018 by Marshall Davis. All rights reserved.

No part of this publication may be reproduced, distributed, or transmitted in any form or by any means, including photocopying, recording, or other electronic or mechanical methods, without the prior written permission of the publisher, except in the case of brief quotations embodied in critical reviews and certain other noncommercial uses permitted by copyright law.

Scripture quotations are from the ESV® Bible (The Holy Bible, English Standard Version®), copyright © 2001 by Crossway, a publishing ministry of Good News Publishers. Used by permission. All rights reserved. May not copy or download more than 500 consecutive verses of the ESV Bible or more than one half of any book of the ESV Bible.

ISBN: 9781730969720

Table of Contents

Christianity Before Beliefs

Once upon a time there was a gospel without doctrines. There was time when Christianity did not have beliefs. It did not require its adherents to accept a set of dogmas or Scriptures. There were no creeds, confessions of faith or doctrinal statements. There were no clergy, priests, or pastors. No vestments or sacraments.

Those features took hundreds of years to gradually evolve. By the fourth century we find a full-fledged religion based on the figure of the crucified and risen savior, Jesus Christ. This was a faith that was prepared to accept its role as the official religion of the Roman Empire, under the benign patronage of its newest convert, Emperor Constantine.

In the beginning Christianity did not even have a name. It was not a religion distinguished from all other religions. It was just a way of life. The early followers of Jesus simply called it "the Way." (Acts 9:2; 19:9, 23; 22:4) The early church was not an institution or an organization. It was a community of pilgrims traveling a spiritual path. That is the way it used to be. It can be that way again.

Is that possible? Can you really have Christianity without all the baggage? Can you be a Christian without beliefs? Can you be a follower of Jesus without believing in concepts like the virgin birth, the deity of Christ, the atonement and the second coming? Sure you can! The original twelve apostles did.

Jesus was not a theologian who taught a systematic theology. He was not a philosopher. He was an untrained, charismatic preacher who taught in the open air of Galilee and Judea. His only education was provided by his parents and the village rabbis of Nazareth, supplemented by brief visits to hear the teachers of the Law in the temple during the annual pilgrimages to Jerusalem for the Jewish feasts.

Jesus left behind no written works. The only thing that Jesus ever wrote were some thoughts scratched into sand while he pondered the fate of a woman accused of adultery. (John 8:8) He certainly did not intend to found a new religion. He did not establish a religious hierarchy. Yet from his teachings emerged the largest religion in world history.

The New Testament gospels are the best evidence we have of Jesus' original teachings. The Synoptic Gospels (Matthew, Mark, and Luke) contain the earliest record of Jesus' teachings. The Sermon on the Mount found in Matthew's gospel is considered to be the essence of Jesus' teaching. It has been called "the greatest sermon ever preached."

The Sermon on the Mount, given at the beginning of his public ministry, encapsulates the basic teachings of Jesus. Because of its nonsectarian tone, adherents of many religions have recognized its greatness. Mahatma Gandhi said of it, "The Sermon on the Mount left a deep impression on my mind when I read it." Later he would write, "Christ's Sermon on the Mount fills me with bliss even today. Its sweet verses have even today the power to quench my agony of soul."

The Sermon on the Mount contains the Christian gospel before it was overshadowed by the teachings of the apostle Paul, a man who never met Jesus or heard him preach. Paul is the true founder of the religion known as Christianity. He transformed the new faith into a set of beliefs, which had to be accepted or else! Paul wrote in one of his earliest letters:

> I am astonished that you are so quickly deserting him who called you in the grace of Christ and are turning to a different gospel — not that there is another one, but there are some who trouble you and want to distort the gospel of Christ. But even if we or an angel from heaven should preach to you a gospel contrary to the one we preached to you, let him be accursed. As we have said before, so now I say again: If anyone is preaching to you

a gospel contrary to the one you received, let him be accursed. (Galatians 1:6-9)

Paul goes on to mention a few verses letter that he did not receive his gospel from the disciples of Jesus. He received it directly from the glorified Christ in a vision. For years he felt no need to have his version of the gospel confirmed by anyone who had actually heard Jesus teach. For Paul, his experience of the risen Christ was self-authenticating. He was right and anyone who disagreed with him on doctrinal matters was accursed. So Christianity, as we know it today, was born.

It would take hundreds of years and a lot of heresy hunting to remove anyone from the church who disagreed with this "orthodox" (meaning "right thinking") position of Paul and his spiritual descendants. But in the end the thought police won. Groups like the Ebionites, who arguably preserved the earliest form of Christianity practiced by the original apostles in Jerusalem, were banned as heretics. The same with the Marcionites and the Gnostics.

Even the Montanists, who were orthodox in doctrine and included the great theologian Tertullian, were ousted. Their heresy was that they allowed the possibility of direct inspiration of ordinary Christians by the Holy Spirit, without going through the hierarchy of church leaders. That was a threat to ecclesiastical authority. Also they included women in church leadership; that was a nonstarter. And so, through struggles with small offshoots and large groups like the Eastern Orthodox and the Protestants, Christianity evolved to the religion we have today.

But in the beginning was Jesus. Jesus' original message can be found in the Sermon on the Mount. In its current form in the Gospel of Matthew, the sermon is meant to evoke parallels to Moses' Book of the Covenant given on Mount Sinai (Exodus 20-23). Whether that was Jesus' intent or the invention of the gospel writer is impossible to tell at this distance from the event. In any case, the Gospel of Matthew cast Jesus in the role of a new Moses.

Jesus proclaims his message on a mountain, just as Moses did. Moses began his instruction with Ten Commandments. Jesus began with Nine Blessings. Jesus reinterprets the ethical laws given by Moses, often quoting them and giving his own interpretation. Whereas Moses was establishing a Law and a religion, Jesus is presenting an alternative to both. Jesus presented a way of spirituality freed from the strictures of religious rules and dogmas. As the Gospel of John says, "The law was given through Moses; grace and truth came through Jesus Christ." (John 1:17)

The first word of the first public teaching of Jesus is the word "blessed." That word encapsulates the difference between the way of

Jesus and the way of religion. Moses began his instruction to the twelve tribes of Israel with a list of demands from God – ten commandments, followed by other laws and rules. Jesus began his sermon to the twelve apostles with nine blessings, followed by a list of ways that his teaching is different from the Law.

Instead of "Thou shalt not" Jesus says, "Blessed art thou." Moses begins with a lists of "do's" and "don'ts." Jesus blesses people just the way they are. In fact he blesses the types of people that we would normally not consider blessed! There is a huge difference between blessing people the way they are and demanding that they change.

Traditional Christianity begins from a position of original sin; Jesus began with original blessing.[1] The Judeo-Christian tradition starts with the proposition that something is fundamentally wrong with human nature. We are sinners. We don't do what we ought to do, and we do what we shouldn't do. The well-known prayer of confession from the Book of Common Prayer voices this mentality:

> "Almighty and most merciful Father; we have erred, and strayed from thy ways like lost sheep. We have followed too much the devices and desires of our own hearts. We have offended against thy holy laws. We have left undone those things which we ought to have done; and we have done those things

which we ought not to have done; and there is no health in us."

That is the Morning Prayer of the Daily Office in the 1928 Book of Common Prayer. That is how the Christian is expected to begin his day. How differently Jesus begins his teaching!

Religion condemns, and then provides a way of redemption. Jesus blesses. Religion digs a hole, pushes you into the hole, and then offers a way out. Jesus assumes that life has enough holes and challenges, and he comforts those who have been wounded by the vicissitudes of life.

Jesus began his Sermon on the Mount with nine blessings (and one call to rejoice).

Blessed are the poor in spirit, for theirs is the kingdom of heaven.
Blessed are those who mourn, for they shall be comforted.
Blessed are the meek, for they shall inherit the earth.
Blessed are those who hunger and thirst for righteousness, for they shall be satisfied.
Blessed are the merciful, for they shall receive mercy.
Blessed are the pure in heart, for they shall see God.
Blessed are the peacemakers, for they shall be called sons of God.

Blessed are those who are persecuted for righteousness' sake, for theirs is the kingdom of heaven.

Blessed are you when others revile you and persecute you and utter all kinds of evil against you falsely on my account.

Rejoice and be glad, for your reward is great in heaven, for so they persecuted the prophets who were before you. (Matthew 5:3-12)

Renunciation

Look at the people whom Jesus blesses. First are the "poor in spirit." "Blessed are the poor in spirit, for theirs is the kingdom of heaven." The version of the beatitudes found in the Gospel of Luke leaves out the phrase "in spirit," indicating that Jesus may have originally been referring to the physically poor. The textual evidence is insufficient to tell if Matthew added the words "in spirit" to Jesus' words or if Luke omitted them.

A third possibility is that Jesus preached different versions of the beatitudes at different times. He likely preached variations of the Sermon on the Mount on different occasions. It is too good of a sermon to only preach once! Preachers today will preach the same sermon to different congregations at different times, changing it to fit the audience and the circumstances. There is no reason to think that Jesus did not do the same thing.

Actually the Sermon on the Mount is most likely not a single sermon but a compilation of his teachings given on many occasions. Even if the Sermon in the Mount as found in the Gospel of Matthew is a transcript of a single message, Jesus undoubtedly preached different versions of this sermon. Luke's gospel contains a very similar "Sermon on the Plain."

For our purposes it does not matter if Jesus said "poor" or "poor in spirit" or both. In the religion of Jesus' day, both the physically and spiritually rich were considered blessed. Those who were poor or "poor in spirit" where not seen as blessed. In either case Jesus' words were revolutionary. Poverty of any kind was understood as a curse in Jesus' day, or at least a sign that one was not blessed by God. The Old Testament repeatedly teaches that material prosperity is a sign of God's favor.

Jesus reverses the curse of this way of thinking. He pronounces a blessing on those people whom the Scriptures would identify as not blessed. Jesus turns the standards of human religion upside down. As Jesus was fond of repeating at every possible opportunity: "The last shall be first and the first last." Take everything you know about religion and invert it, and you have the spiritual teaching of Jesus.

If Jesus actually used the phrase "poor in spirit" (if the qualifier was not added later by a scribe looking for a loophole) then Jesus probably meant developing an attitude of poverty. We could also call it an attitude of renunciation.

Those who did not have the faith to literally renounce all possessions could still change their attitude toward what they owned. They could decide not allow their possessions to possess them. They could practice an attitude of detachment from worldly things. They could be "poor in spirit," even while possessing material things. This is a call to live simply in a society that idolizes wealth.

This is the best way for American Christians to receive Jesus' blessing. I doubt that readers of this book will take Jesus' advice to the rich young ruler and "go and sell all you possess and give to the poor, and you will have treasure in heaven; and come, follow Me." (Mark 10:21) Our society does not provide for religious mendicants in the way that ancient societies did. But we can still take Jesus' teaching about being "poor in spirit" seriously.

We can cultivate a counter-cultural attitude of detachment from material things. We can refuse to be defined as "consumers." We can simplify our lifestyles. We can reject the materialistic mindset of our culture, which judges a person's worth by salary, clothing, housing, and possession of the newest technology. We can downsize. We can find our identity, not in the materialistic values of our culture, but in the spiritual values of the Kingdom of God. That is what it means to be poor in spirit.

Impermanence

Jesus goes on to bless those who grieve. "Blessed are those who mourn, for they shall be comforted." Loss is the abiding reality of life. As the author of the Pastoral Epistles teaches, we brought nothing into this world and we can take nothing from it. (I Timothy 6:7) Nothing is permanent. Eventually we will lose everything we have gained throughout our lives, whether it be possessions, family, health, youth, beauty, strength, mental acuity, or anything else. Finally we lose our lives. This litany of loss is the subject of the existential meditation known as the Book of Ecclesiastes. It causes the "Preacher" to cry out "Vanity, vanity, all is vanity!" Life is impermanent.

Everything decays. The law of entropy is unavoidable. Everything that is born dies. Death is one of the realities of life that modern science has not been able to conquer. Grief is the emotional response to such loss. Even though we have extended the average human life span by decades and reduced infant mortality, death still finds us and those we love.

In my experience as a pastor, I have seen firsthand that death is dreaded by Christians and non-Christians alike. We do everything we can to ignore death, mask death or hide its ugly face, but it always slips past our defenses. People, whether they want to or not, grieve. In my experience most Americans grieve badly, without the established customs of traditional societies to help them manage the grief.

Loss hurts. Mourning does not feel like a blessing to us. It feels like a curse. Indeed the Bible labels death as a curse laid upon Adam and Eve's descendants by God as punishment for their primordial disobedience. But Jesus reverses the curse. He declares that those who mourn are blessed. "Blessed are those who mourn, for they shall be comforted." How can this be? What is the comfort he speaks of?

The spirituality of Jesus sees mourning in a new light. It is embraced as a path to peace and wisdom. As the psalmist writes, "Teach us to number our days, that we may gain a heart of wisdom." (Psalm 90:12) Loss is integral to life. Death is the flip side of birth, two sides of the same coin. If death is inevitable, and there is nothing we can do to stop it, then one may as well accept it. Embrace it and find the blessing at its heart.

It is a part of Buddhist practice to meditate upon one's own death. It was one of the "four sights" of Siddhartha Gautama (known as the Buddha), which prompted his spiritual quest for enlightenment. A Buddhist novice is expected to visit a cemetery and meditate on the transience of life and the inevitability of death.

Death is also at core of Christian spirituality. The symbol of Christianity is the Cross – an instrument of death. Memento mori (Latin, meaning "remember death") is the medieval Christian practice of reflecting on mortality. Ars moriendi ("The Art of Dying") is a spiritual practice (and Latin text) of the 15th century, which instructs Christians how to live well in the light of death.

In the case of Jesus, death came in the form of an early, unjust, and violent end. We worship a crucified Lord who called us to take up our cross and follow him unto death. Yet Christians usually do not take up the cross and embrace death as part of faith. We do not see losing everything as a blessing. Quite the contrary. The average Christian does everything possible to avoid suffering and death. It seems to me that Christians fear death just as much as non-Christians. Most Christians have come to terms with death or embraced the way of the cross.

How is mourning a blessing? Mourning is a powerful emotional reminder of the truth at the heart of the universe - that life is brief and its end is certain. There will come a time when each of us will lose everything that we have and are. That is true whether we are the one who survives the death of a loved one or the one who dies.

We were made from nothing (*ex nihilo* is the Latin phrase Christian theologians use) and we return to nothing. We are dust and to dust we shall return. The physical body, which we take such pains to protect and preserve, will return to the earth. The personal reputation that we carefully cultivate will be forgotten. Even our distinctive human personality, which we mistake for our true selves, will disappear. It is merely a product of the brain; our psyche dies with the body. Mourning brings us face to face with the uncomfortable reality of nonexistence.

In July 46 BC, Julius Caesar was at the height of his power and popularity. He was returning to Rome after a very successful military campaign to extend Rome's borders. It is reported that as he entered Rome to the roar of cheering citizens, he instructed one of his slaves to stand in his chariot beside him and repeat these phrases in his ear: "Remember, thou are but a man" and "This, too, will pass."

Our essence – if you want to call it that – is impermanence. Everything we have and are is transitory. This is the uncomfortable truth that religion obfuscates with its doctrines of immortal souls, repeated rebirths, and eternal afterlives. Only when we ground our identity in the reality of impermanence will we find the comfort that we seek. That is what Jesus promises in this blessing.

Is there life beyond death? I hope there is. That is what Christianity teaches. I believe there is. Then again, it is natural to believe one is immortal. Studies cited by *Scientific American* reveal that it is common for people to think that their minds continue on after they die, regardless of their religious beliefs.[2] Indeed it seems to be impossible for a human being to imagine not existing.

Sigmund Freud wrote a century ago, "It is indeed impossible to imagine our own death; and whenever we attempt to do so we can perceive that we are in fact still present as spectators."[3] He concludes, "At bottom no one believes in his own death.... In the unconscious every one of us is convinced of his own immortality." The poet Edward Young put it this way: "All men think all men mortal, but themselves." As American comedian Steven Wright said, "I intend to live forever. So far, so good."[4]

If there is life beyond death, I suspect it is not as individual personalities. Our psychological identity must necessarily die with our physical bodies. How could it possibly be otherwise? How could we think without a brain or feel without a nervous system? Where would our memories be stored? Without the physical structure of the brain, the human identities based on that structure cease.

What continues beyond physical death is the nonmaterial Life of God, which Jesus calls the Kingdom of Heaven. We return to the Life we had before our birth. We recover the original face we had before our parents were born, as the koan says. This is life after death. It is the Life that gave birth to the universe and still beats at the heart of the universe. It is the eternal life of God.

The Teacher of Ecclesiastes called it Emptiness. (Ecclesiastes 1:2) It is his term for the nameless God, the one who identified himself to Moses as "I am." It is not nothingness; it is a full emptiness. It is not non-existence; it is Being. It is the Womb from which the universe was birthed.

Eternity beyond and behind this cosmic play of transience is the only reality that never dies. Only when we discover our identity in this reality will we find the comfort we seek. As the Upanishads say, "That thou art." This is not a doctrine to be believed, but a reality to be experienced. Only when this is experientially known does comfort come, the peace that transcends understanding. (Philippians 4:7) It is only by embracing the heart of mourning that we apprehend this truth that does not die. Blessed are those who mourn, for they shall be comforted.

Humility

The world belongs to the strong. The alpha male leads the pack or the tribe, whether it be human or animal. Evolution favors the strong. Survival of the fittest, "Nature, red in tooth and claw." It is the bold who rise to the top of the social hierarchy to lead kingdoms and empires. The meek are victims trodden underfoot. That is the conventional wisdom of the world.

Jesus reverses this natural order of things. He says, "Blessed are the meek, for they shall inherit the earth." It doesn't make sense and doesn't ring true to personal experience. History is not made by the cautious. On the other hand there are some advantages to laying low. As the saying goes, "The early bird catches the worm, but the second mouse gets the cheese."

When it comes to the spiritual life, the ways of the world do not work. Once again, the last shall be first and the first last. Many are called, but few are chosen. In the Kingdom of God the last ones standing are the meek. Who exactly are the meek?

It is a slippery term. Meek does not mean weak, though it may be manifested through weakness. The apostle Paul writes of his personal infirmity,

> So to keep me from becoming conceited because of the surpassing greatness of the revelations, a thorn was given me in the flesh, a messenger of Satan to harass me, to keep me from becoming conceited. Three times I pleaded with the Lord about this, that it should leave me. But he said to me, "My grace is sufficient for you, for my power is made perfect in weakness." Therefore I will boast all the more gladly of my weaknesses, so that the power of Christ may rest upon me. For the sake of Christ, then, I am content with weaknesses, insults, hardships, persecutions, and calamities. For when I am weak, then I am strong. (2 Corinthians 12:7-10)

For Paul, God's power is made perfect in weakness. Physical weakness was an opportunity for spiritual strength to be manifested. Jesus was ignominiously executed on a Roman cross. Yet the gospel born from that weakness conquered the mighty Roman Empire. The meek Christians, who refused to lift a hand against their enemies, conquered the greatest military empire of the Western world. They literally inherited the earth - at least that portion of the earth.

Meekness is the strength of weakness. Meekness is grounded in self-denial. Jesus said, "If anyone would come after me, let him deny himself and take up his cross and follow me. For whoever would save his life will lose it, but whoever loses his life for my sake will find it. For what will it profit a man if he gains the whole world and forfeits his soul? Or what shall a man give in return for his soul? (Matthew 16:24-26)

Meekness takes the low road. Lao Tzu speaks about the meekness of water, which always seeks the lowest place because it is its nature.

Goodness is like water,
which gives life to all living things.
It assumes the lowest places,
and is like God. (Tao Te Ching 8)

A Christian interpretation of the Tao Te Ching links this to the meekness of Christ:

Christ takes the lowest place,
and is exalted to the highest place.
He is not attached to earthly things,
and therefore enjoys all things.
He empties himself,
and is thereby complete. (Tao Te Ching, 7)

The "meekness" of water conquers the hardest rock and shapes the landscape of the earth, according to this classic Chinese book of wisdom:

Nothing is gentler than water,
yet nothing is more effective
at wearing away hard rock.
Nothing is greater than God
in overcoming hard times.

Weakness conquers strength.
The flexible overcomes the rigid.
Everyone knows this,
but no one practices this.

Therefore Christ says,
"Whoever wants to be great
must be a servant to all,
and whoever wants to be first
must be last of all." (Tao Te Ching 78) [5]

The power of meekness is born from a radical understanding and experience of self. Self-denial is not the suppression of one's wants and desires, as is commonly supposed. It is not a pathological denigration of oneself which kowtows to others because of a deficiency of self-worth. Self-denial is an experiential awareness of no-self. It is the awareness that there is no permanent self. From an eternal perspective, the human self is a transitory phenomenon and not our true nature. That is the root of spiritual self-denial.

This is a radical statement when made in the context of Western individualism. Western culture elevates the self above all else. It believes that every psychological and social problem can be cured by a healthy dose of self-esteem. Western philosophy is grounded in Descartes' foundational assertion "Cogito, ergo sum," "I think, therefore I am." For most people, if there is one thing we can be sure of, it is that we are. Jesus suggests otherwise.

A simple examination of one's own life will reveal the illusory nature of the self. Physically we are not the same person we were as children. It is said that every cell in our bodies is replaced every seven years. We are not who we were a few years ago. If we are not our bodies, then we are not our gender, race, or nationality.

Furthermore we are not our thoughts. Our views on all sorts of matters change over the years. Our beliefs change. Our political views can change, as can our religion. Our emotions change. A simple meditation exercise reveals that our emotions are nothing more than energy flowing through our bodies. They ebb and flow through our brains and limbs like waves crashing on a beach.

Even our memories change. We have a sense of being the same person we were as a child because we have a lifetime of memories. But studies have known how unreliable our memories are. Memories are continually being edited by our brains to fit our newest story of who we are. Steven Novella, a clinical neurologist at Yale University School of Medicine writes:

"But how reliable is human memory? Think of a vivid childhood remembrance, the kind of memory that you recall often and that represents an important part of your history and identity. I hate to break this to you (actually, no I don't), but that memory is probably mostly, or even entirely, fake. You may find that notion disturbing, and right now you are thinking, "No way. I clearly remember that trip to the toy store when I was ten. No way is it fake." But, I'm sorry to say, a century of memory research is not on your side. Our memories aren't accurate or passive recordings of the past. We don't have squishy camcorders in our skulls. Memories are constructed from imperfect perceptions filtered through our beliefs and biases, and then over time they morph and merge. Our memories serve more to support our beliefs than to inform them. In a way, they are an evolving story we tell ourselves."[6]

The brain, which we assume is the receptacle of our permanent selves, is malleable. It can be very unreliable at times. Brains, like any other organ, are subject to disease and old age. Everyone who has had firsthand experience of persons with Alzheimer's disease, or other forms of dementia and memory loss, know how a person's "self" can be devastated by disease.

Our loved ones are not who they once were. Neither are we.

We are not ourselves. We are not our "self." We are not our thoughts, our beliefs, our emotions, or our memories. Even though we sense a continuity with our past selves, we are not who we were mentally, emotionally or physically.

We are not who we think we are. We think we are distinct psychological entities inhabiting physical bodies. We are under the illusion that there is something permanent about us. Something that has remained the same since our physical birth and which - we hope and pray - will continue after our physical death. It is not true. The only truth is impermanence. We are not our self. There is no self.

Meekness is living out this reality. It is embracing the reality of not-self. That is the root of Christian self-denial. That is what it means to deny oneself, pick up the cross and follow Jesus. The apostle Paul wrote, "I have been crucified with Christ. It is no longer I who live, but Christ who lives in me." (Galatians 2:20) Paul had been to the cross, spiritually speaking. He had experienced the death of the self. He realized that he no longer lived. There was only Christ, who is God. This was the essence of Christ's experience according to Paul. He wrote:

> "Have this mind among yourselves, which is yours in Christ Jesus, who,

though he was in the form of God, did not count equality with God a thing to be grasped, but emptied himself, by taking the form of a servant, being born in the likeness of men. And being found in human form, he humbled himself by becoming obedient to the point of death, even death on a cross. Therefore God has highly exalted him and bestowed on him the name that is above every name, so that at the name of Jesus every knee should bow, in heaven and on earth and under the earth, and every tongue confess that Jesus Christ is Lord, to the glory of God the Father." (Philippians 2:5-11)

According to Paul Christ "emptied himself" and in so doing he was exalted. The Meek One inherited the heavens and earth! That is exactly what Jesus was talking about in the beatitude when he said, "Blessed are the meek, for they shall inherit the earth." Christ is the definition of meekness.

Perseverance

A young man came to a hermit, who was renowned for his holiness. He said, "O great teacher, I come to you seeking wisdom." "Come with me," the holy man replied, "and I will baptize you." "But I have already been baptized," the man asserted. "Come with me," the monk insisted. He led him down to a river and took him chest deep into the water. Then he asked him, "What do you want?" "Wisdom, O holy one," said the young man.

The holy man put his strong hands on the man's shoulders and pushed him under. Thirty seconds later he let him up. "What do you want?" he asked again. "Wisdom," the young man sputtered, "O great and wise one." He pushed him under again. Thirty seconds, thirty-five, forty – and then he let him up. The man was coughing. "What do you want, young man?"

Between heavy breaths the fellow wheezed, "Wisdom! O wise and wonderful..." The monk jammed him under again – forty seconds passed then fifty – then he let him up. "What do you want?" "Air!" the young man gasped. "I need air!" "Good!" the holy man replied. "When you want wisdom as much as air, you will find it."

Jesus said, "Blessed are those who hunger and thirst for righteousness, for they shall be satisfied." Only those who hunger and thirst for God the way a drowning man needs air, a hungry man craves food, and a thirsty man desires water, will find God.

Later in the Sermon on the Mount Jesus said, "Keep on asking, and you will receive what you ask for. Keep on seeking, and you will find. Keep on knocking, and the door will be opened to you." (Matthew 7:7 New Living Translation) Persistence is the key factor. "Pray without ceasing" was the Apostle Paul's advice.

Most people do not hunger for spiritual food. They are content with dawdling in the outer court enjoying the aromas of holiness wafting from the Holy of Holies. Most religious people play at the spiritual life. They are not serious about it. They do not need truth to live. They are not willing to give up everything - families, wealth, security ... even their own selves - for truth. But only those who need God the way a man in the desert needs water will find God.

Jesus told a story of persistent woman. Here is a contemporary retelling of the parable entitled "The Single Mom Who Wouldn't Quit."

> There was a city judge who apathetic about everyone and everything - including God. In that same city there was a single mom who appeared before his court repeatedly, always seeking justice

against the same sleazy landlord. He always dismissed her cases. After a while he said to himself, "I will give this woman the justice she desires. Not because I care about her or believe that God cares, but because she is clogging up my docket." Jesus then explained, "See what this apathetic judge did? Will not a caring God give justice to his people who pray fervently to him 24/ 7? Do you think God will ignore their pleas? No! He will act swiftly to ensure that justice is done. Yet when the Messiah comes, will he find faith on earth? (Luke 18: 1– 8)[7]

Only the person who persists in the spiritual life, receives. The Gospel of Matthew tells the story of Jesus encountering another desperate woman.

Jesus went away from there and withdrew to the district of Tyre and Sidon. And behold, a Canaanite woman from that region came out and was crying, "Have mercy on me, O Lord, Son of David; my daughter is severely oppressed by a demon." But he did not answer her a word. And his disciples came and begged him, saying, "Send her away, for she is crying out after us." He answered, "I was sent only to the lost sheep of the house of Israel." But she came and knelt before him, saying, "Lord, help me." And he answered, "It is not right to take the children's bread and throw it to the dogs." She said, "Yes, Lord, yet even the dogs eat the crumbs that fall from their masters' table." Then Jesus answered her, "O woman, great is your faith! Be it done for you as you desire." And her daughter was healed instantly. (Matthew 15:21-28)

This woman was willing to endure any abuse – including being called a dog by the Messiah – in order to gain healing for her daughter. That is how much she loved her child. Jesus said, "If you then, who are evil, know how to give good gifts to your children, how much more will the heavenly Father give the Holy Spirit to those who ask him!" (Luke 11:13) Elsewhere he predicted "the love of many will grow cold, but he who perseveres to the end will be saved." (Matthew 24:13)

One must love God more than anything else in life in order to find God. Jesus said, "Whoever loves father or mother more than me is not worthy of me, and whoever loves son or daughter more than me is not worthy of me. And whoever does not take his cross and follow me is not worthy of me. Whoever finds his life will lose it, and whoever loses his life for my sake will find it." Matthew 10:37-39)

A rich young man came to Jesus seeking eternal life. He was willing to do anything except give up his wealth. When Jesus asked him to do that, "the young man … went away sorrowful, for he had great possessions." (Matthew 19:22)

Most of us have an Achilles heel, a spiritually fatal flaw, a price we are unwilling to pay to gain the Kingdom of God. Only when we persist through every obstacle and are willing to give up everything for the spiritual life, will the door to the Kingdom open. All the great spiritual teachers of the ages gave up everything for the spiritual quest. The Buddha called it "right intention" or "right effort" (samma vayama) as part of his eightfold path.

Persistence. Perseverance. The one who perseveres to the end is Joseph Campbell's "hero with a thousand faces" of ancient myths and legends. Only those who persevere through all obstacles reach their goal. The apostle Paul writes, "For I am already being poured out as a drink offering, and the time of my departure has come. I have fought the good fight, I have finished the race, I have kept the faith. Henceforth there is laid up for me the crown of righteousness, which the Lord, the righteous judge, will award to me on that day, and not only to me but also to all who have loved his appearing." (2 Timothy 4:7-8)

Compassion

"Blessed are the merciful, for they shall receive mercy." Mercy is the gracious attitude of those with power toward those who do not have power. A king is able to extend mercy to his subjects. A judge is able to extend mercy to the criminal. The rich are able to extend mercy – in the form of alms – to those who are poor. Mercy is the power of the powerful. That would include spiritual power. Another word for this willingness to extend mercy is compassion.

The Gospel of Matthew says of Jesus, "When he saw the crowds, he had compassion for them, because they were harassed and helpless, like sheep without a shepherd." (Matthew 9:36) It says later, "When he went ashore he saw a great crowd, and he had compassion on them and healed their sick." (Matthew 14:14) "Then Jesus called his disciples to him and said, "I have compassion on the crowd because they have been with me now three days and have nothing to eat. And I am unwilling to send them away hungry, lest they faint on the way." (Matthew 15:32)

Compassion was one of the hallmarks of Jesus' ministry. The word "compassion" literally means "to feel with" or "to suffer with." One with compassion imagines himself in the position of one in need and reaches out to help. When we have compassion for those who are poor, we imagine ourselves in the shoes of the poor and ask what we would want and need. Then we provide it. "In everything, then, do to others as you would have them do to you. For this is the essence of the Law and the prophets." (Matthew 6:12)

Jesus taught that true spirituality is to feed the hungry, clothe the naked, care for the sick, visit the prisoners, and welcome the stranger. For insomuch as we do it for the least of these Jesus' sisters and brothers, we do it to him. (Matthew 25:35-46) James says, "Religion that is pure and undefiled before God the Father is this: to visit orphans and widows in their affliction, and to keep oneself unstained from the world. (James 1:27)

Compassion can take the form of political and social action on behalf of the poor. It means to house the homeless and provide healthcare for the sick. It means to welcome the stranger. The spirituality of Jesus was not an inward obsession with individual salvation. It was directed outward to those in need.

The earliest gospel in the New Testament canon is the Gospel of Mark. It contains very little preaching or teaching by Jesus. In Mark's gospel the Kingdom of God is demonstrated through actions. Jesus spends the majority of this time in this gospel exercising spiritual power on behalf of those in need. It pictures Jesus as one with authority over disease and "unclean spirits." Jesus is portrayed not as a teacher of spiritual truth but as one who exercised spiritual power. He is a healer and exorcist. Demons and unclean spirits were the first century explanation for mental illness, as well as physical illnesses like epilepsy. Jesus freed people from their power; he was a healthcare provider.

This ministry of healing was inspired by compassion. "He was preaching in their synagogues throughout all Galilee, and casting out demons. Now a leper came to Him, imploring Him, kneeling down to Him and saying to Him, 'If You are willing, You can make me clean.' Then Jesus, moved with compassion, stretched out His hand and touched him, and said to him, 'I am willing; be cleansed.' As soon as He had spoken, immediately the leprosy left him, and he was cleansed." (Mark 1:39-42 NKJV)

When compassion permeates a culture it takes the form of social ministry and social justice. In American spirituality it is popular to separate the "spiritual" from the physical. Indeed today there is a new movement that demonizes the "social gospel," which focuses on physical human needs. In a Sunday morning sermon on August 26, 2018, the influential Reformed pastor John MacArthur, acknowledged by *Christianity Today* as one of the most influential preachers of our time,[8] repudiated the social gospel as a heresy.

He wrote a couple of weeks earlier in an August 13 blog, "Evangelicalism's newfound obsession with the notion of "social justice" is a significant shift — and I'm convinced it's a shift that is moving many people (including some key evangelical leaders) off message, and onto a trajectory that many other movements and denominations have taken before, always with spiritually disastrous results." He writes, "Over the years, I've fought a number of polemical battles against ideas that threaten the gospel. This recent (and surprisingly sudden) detour in quest of 'social justice' is, I believe, the most subtle and dangerous threat so far." [9]

With MacArthur's backing, over 9000 evangelicals and Reformed Christians signed a document condemning social justice, entitled simply "The Statement on Social Justice & the Gospel." According to the introduction to the document, it is designed to "to clarify certain key Christian doctrines and ethical principles prescribed in God's Word" in order to "withstand an onslaught of dangerous and false teachings that threaten the gospel, misrepresent Scripture, and lead people away from the grace of God in Jesus Christ." It goes on to say, "If the doctrines of God's Word are not uncompromisingly reasserted and defended ..., there is every reason to anticipate that these dangerous ideas and corrupted moral values will spread their influence into other realms of biblical doctrines and principles."[10]

This statement is an example of modern Christians who are obsessed with doctrine and religion and have abandoned the gospel of Jesus. They have forgotten what Christianity was like before creeds. There is no division in the Bible or in Jesus' ministry between social justice and the gospel. The Old Testament prophets were preoccupied with justice for the poor and oppressed. The prophet Amos castigated Israel for being obsessed with religious worship while ignoring social justice.

> Thus says the Lord:
> "For three transgressions of Israel,
>   and for four, I will not revoke the
>   punishment,
> because they sell the righteous for silver,
>   and the needy for a pair of sandals—
> those who trample the head of the poor into
>   the dust of the earth
>   and turn aside the way of the afflicted.
>   (Amos 2:6-7)

He goes on to say later:

> I hate, I despise your feasts,
>   and I take no delight in your solemn
>   assemblies.
> Even though you offer me your burnt
>   offerings and grain offerings,
>   I will not accept them;

and the peace offerings of your fattened
   animals,
   I will not look upon them.
Take away from me the noise of your songs;
   to the melody of your harps I will not
   listen.
But let justice roll down like waters,
   and righteousness like an ever-flowing
   stream." (Amos 5:21-24)

When Jesus inaugurated his public ministry
he described it as the fulfillment of the words of
the prophet Isaiah.

"The Spirit of the Lord is upon me,
   because he has anointed me
   to proclaim good news to the poor.
He has sent me to proclaim liberty to the
   captives
   and recovering of sight to the blind,
   to set at liberty those who are oppressed,
to proclaim the year of the Lord's favor."
   (Luke 4:18-19, Isaiah 49:8-9)

Those who wish to recover the spirit of Jesus'
original prophetic gospel and ministry must
reject this message of division proclaimed by the
evangelical and Reformed Christians who signed
"The Statement on Social Justice & the Gospel."
If Mark's gospel is correct, Jesus spent much
more time healing than he did preaching. His
ministry was one of compassion for those in

physical need. Those who wish to follow Jesus today must do the same. As Francis of Assisi is reported to have said, "Preach the gospel at all times. If necessary, use words."

Inwardness

For the first thirty years of his life, Jesus was a private person. Except for a brief episode when he was twelve years old, we know virtually nothing about his life before he began his ministry at about the age of thirty. By the time he had become a public figure, he had already established a personal habit of spiritual discipline, which we can assume was the pattern throughout his earlier adult life.

He began his ministry with a forty day solitary retreat in the wilderness. During his ministry he used to get off by himself, as often as he could, for silence and solitude. He was a man used to private communion with God. Therefore it is not surprising that he speaks about the inner life of the heart in this sermon. In the Beatitudes he refers to the process of inner purification by which one comes to see God, saying, "Blessed are the pure in heart, for they shall see God."

This is spiritual sight accomplished through spiritual discipline. He is referring to the inward journey of the soul, which Evelyn Underhill calls "the Mystic Way" in her classic work on Christian mysticism.[11] Jesus spoke of the "secret place" or the "inner room" in reference to prayer. (6:6) It was a reference to the innermost chamber – the Holy of Holies – of the temple, but Jesus was speaking metaphorically. Only priests could go physically into the Holy Place of the temple, and only the high priest could go into the Holy of Holies. But anyone could go into the holy of holies of the human soul.

Jesus was speaking of the inner chamber of the spiritual heart. It is a place of silence and solitude, a spiritual place that Jesus visited often. He called it by the biblical term "heart." This is a term used throughout the Old Testament and New Testament to refer to the innermost recesses of the human soul.

Jesus taught no meditation technique to his disciples, but he was a man of natural contemplative prayer that brought him into the presence of his Heavenly Father. It is through inward spiritual practice that one purifies the heart and becomes aware of the Divine Presence. As the psalmist said, "Be still and know that I am God." (Psalm 46:10) This is the "still small voice" of God, (better translated the "sound of silence") experienced by the prophet Elijah. (I Kings 19:12)

This is the experience of spiritual practitioners throughout the centuries. The 13th-century Sufi mystic Rumi said, "Let the waters settle and you will see the moon and the stars mirrored in your own being." Lao Tzu wrote, "How does one make muddy water clear? Be still, and the water will clear in time. How does one become still? Let everything happen, and stillness appears."[12]

Jesus spoke of this inward journey metaphorically. When he told the parable of the prodigal son, he was speaking of a figurative "far country" that the son went to. When the son returned home, he was coming back to "his Father's house," which was the term Jesus used for the Kingdom of God, as well as the temple.

When Jesus spoke of the Kingdom of God growing like a mustard seed, he was speaking of the slow and quiet process of spiritual growth. When he talked about seed falling on different types of soil, he was referring to the soil of the soul. Even though Jesus was not a farmer, many of his metaphors came from agriculture, because it lent itself much better to the spiritual life than his occupation as a carpenter.

Even the gospel accounts of Jesus' public ministry can be interpreted as an allegorical journey of the soul. He travels throughout the countryside, and even ventures outside of the Holy Land. But the story ends in Jerusalem, which was considered by Jews to be the physical and spiritual center of the world. There in the Holy City, the home of the House of God, Jesus dies and is resurrected. The gospel narrative is an allegory of the spiritual life. Jesus was acting out a spiritual teaching, like prophets did in the

Old Testament. One comes to the Center and dies to self in order to be reborn through the power of God as a transformed, "resurrected" human being.

The spiritual life is an inward life. It is also an outward life of service and ministry. But the outer journey is fed by the inner journey. Jesus often refreshed his soul in times of silence and solitude in order to find strength for the journey. In the same way we follow him on this journey of inward discovery. In the silence of inner stillness, the dust of the journey falls away. Our hearts are purified in the presence of the Holy One, and we see God.

To see God is to have an intimate, mystical awareness of God. In the Old Testament there were only two people who ever "saw God." There was Jacob, who in his wrestling match at the Jabbok river "saw God face to face." (Genesis 32:30) He was transformed and renamed Israel and became the progenitor of the Jews. The other person was Moses, who talked to God in the Tent of Meeting "face to face as a man speaks to a friend." (Exodus 33:11)

We can interpret those as visionary experiences. There are other such experiences in Scripture. The prophet Isaiah speaks of seeing the Lord in a vision "seated on a throne high and lifted up." John of Patmos saw God seated on his throne in the Book of Revelation. To see God is to have a visionary or mystical encounter with

God. This is what Jesus is referring to in this beatitude. That spiritual experience comes as a result of purifying one's heart.

James says, "Come near to God and he will come near to you.... purify your hearts, you double-minded." (James 4:8) The psalmist sang, "Create in me a pure heart, O God, and renew a steadfast spirit within me." (Psalm 51:10) The apostle Paul writes, "Dear friends, let us purify ourselves from everything that contaminates body and spirit, perfecting holiness out of reverence for God." (2 Corinthians 7:1 NIV)

The spiritual life is an invitation to an inward journey of purification through the spiritual discipline of silence and solitude, where one dwells in the presence of God in quiet contemplation. In the process one's heart is purified, and one awakens to the Presence of God. The pure in heart shall see God.

Peacemaking

Jesus was a peacemaker. That is why he was called the Son of God. "Blessed are the peacemakers, for they shall be called sons of God." In the Sermon on the Mount Jesus called his disciples to peacemaking. And he practiced what he preached. Jesus sought to bring together segments of society that had become alienated due to religious rules of morality and purity.

He was accused by his detractors of "eating with tax collectors and sinners." He was known for welcoming those whom society had rejected, forming them into a new community, which he created to be a reflection of his Father's Kingdom, so that God's will might be done "on earth as it is in heaven." He willingly incorporated the misfits of the world into his spiritual community.

He was a reconciler. When informed of religious competitors ministering in his name who were not part of his group, he said, "Whoever is not against us is for us" (Luke 9:50). His apostles tried to get a member of a rival group to "cease and desist," Jesus said, "Do not stop him, for no one who does a mighty work in my name will be able soon afterward to speak evil of me. For the one who is not against us is for us." (Mark 9:39-40)

He was not a stickler for uniformity. He had no desire to exercise his authority over people. He welcomed all. But he reserved his harshest words for religious people who erected barriers to the inclusion of people. He drew his circle of spiritual community wide.

This attitude of inclusion and reconciliation became part of Pauline Christianity. Paul (probably quoting an early baptismal formula) says, "For in Christ Jesus you are all sons of God, through faith. For as many of you as were baptized into Christ have put on Christ. There is neither Jew nor Greek, there is neither slave nor free, there is no male and female, for you are all one in Christ Jesus." (Galatians 3:26-28) He wrote, "If it is possible, as far as it depends on you, live at peace with everyone." (Romans 1218)

Christian ministry is patterned on Jesus' ministry of reconciliation. 2 Corinthians 5:18 says, "All this is from God, who through Christ reconciled us to himself and gave us the ministry of reconciliation." We are to be peacemakers, reconciling people to one another and to God. Our world naturally divides into tribal groups – political, national, religious, and ethnic tribes - who exclude each other, demonize each other, and even kill each other. In the place of these fiefdoms of exclusion Jesus proclaims the Kingdom of God, which knows no such categories.

In the "Revelation of Jesus Christ" John has a vision of this kingdom, which includes all peoples, not just "the people of God," which were described in a scene immediately before. "After this I looked, and behold, a great multitude that no one could number, from every nation, from all tribes and peoples and languages, standing before the throne and before the Lamb, clothed in white robes, with palm branches in their hands, and crying out with a loud voice, 'Salvation belongs to our God who sits on the throne, and to the Lamb!'" (Revelation 7:9-10)

The peaceable kingdom has been accomplished through Christ, who is himself the embodiment of peace. "For he himself is our peace, who has made the two one and has broken down in his flesh the dividing wall of hostility by abolishing the law of commandments expressed in ordinances, that he might create in himself one new man in place of the two, so making peace, and might reconcile us both to God in one body through the cross, thereby killing the hostility. And he came and preached peace to you who were far off and peace to those who were near." (Ephesians 2:14-17)

Outward peacemaking is a manifestation of inner peace. Two can become one in the Kingdom of God because the two have become one in us. Jew and Gentile become one. Male and female become one. Even God and human become one in Christ. We become one with God and each other as Jesus prayed we would.

> "I do not ask for these only, but also for those who will believe in me through their word, that they may all be one, just as you, Father, are in me, and I in you, that they also may be in us, so that the world may believe that you have sent me. The glory that you have given me I have given to them, that they may be one even as we are one, I in them and you in me, that they may become perfectly one, so that the world may know that you sent me and loved them even as you loved me. (John 17:20-23)

Jesus is talking about unity with God. We are one with God. This oneness is not a theological statement. This is a description of Christian experience. We can experience the "peace of God that transcends human understanding." We can know union with God and all of God's creation. Paul says that God is "over all and through all and in all." (Ephesians 4:6) We can know personally. Oneness with God, which Jesus and Paul speaks about, is not a theological abstraction. It is an experiential reality.

The Gospel of Thomas is as early as any of the canonical gospels of our New Testament. In it Jesus speaks the familiar words that we have to become like children to enter the Kingdom of God. Then he adds some further words:

Jesus saw some infants who were being suckled. He said to his disciples: These infants being suckled are like those who enter the kingdom. They said to him: If we then become children, shall we enter the kingdom? Jesus said to them: When you make the two one, and when you make the inside as the outside, and the outside as the inside, and the upper as the lower, and when you make the male and the female into a single one, so that the male is not male and the female not female, and when you make eyes in place of an eye, and a hand in place of a hand, and a foot in place of a foot, an image in place of an image, then shall you enter the kingdom. (Gospel of Thomas 22)

The wording of this non-canonical gospel may sound strange to our ears, which is so accustomed to the familiar phrases of the New Testament. But it is really just talking about this same type of oneness within oneself and with God. Oneness is peace. It is reconciliation within oneself and others as well as God.

Peace begins from within. As the song says, "Let there be peace on earth and let it begin with me." We cannot be peacemakers in the world unless we are at peace in our inner world. Orthodox Christianity has focused mainly on peace with God, saying "We have peace with God through our Lord Jesus Christ." (Romans 5:1) We need to reclaim our birthright of inner peace as well. Jesus said, "The Kingdom of God is within you." This is the peace of unity within oneself.

It is because Jesus had inner peace that he can be our peace. When we are united within ourselves and with Christ and God, then we share in this universal peace, which is the essence of creation. "And the peace of God, which surpasses all understanding, will guard your hearts and your minds in Christ Jesus." (Philippians 4:7) When we have peace, then we can pass that peace on to others. We can be ministers of peace and reconciliation in the world. Then we will be are called sons of God.

Persecution

The spirituality of Jesus is countercultural. His teachings are a challenge to the monopoly of established religion and the hegemony of the state. That is why these worldly forces arrested and executed him. He was viewed as blasphemous and treasonous. The same is true for his followers. According to the Gospel of John Jesus said, "If the world hates you, keep in mind that it hated me first. If you belonged to the world, it would love you as its own. As it is, you do not belong to the world, but I have chosen you out of the world. That is why the world hates you. Remember what I told you: 'A servant is not greater than his master.' If they persecuted me, they will persecute you also." (John 15:18-20 NIV)

In the last two of the Nine Blessings, Jesus deals with this theme. "Blessed are those who are persecuted for righteousness' sake, for theirs is the kingdom of heaven. Blessed are you when others revile you and persecute you and utter all kinds of evil against you falsely on my account. Rejoice and be glad, for your reward is great in heaven, for so they persecuted the prophets who were before you." (Matthew 5:10-12)

The persecution of spiritual nonconformists is present in all cultures, but is particularly prevalent in societies with an authoritarian religious structure. In September 2018 Coptic Christians were nominated for the Nobel Peace Prize for their practice of peacemaking and nonviolence. They refused to retaliate against lethal persecution from governments and terrorist groups in Egypt and elsewhere. According to a 2018 report by the Christian charity *Open Doors*, Christians in Egypt face 'unprecedented levels of persecution.' Last year, according to the report, "128 Egyptian Christians were killed for their faith and more than 200 were driven out of their homes." The organization said, "Despite this, Coptic Christians have consistently refused to retaliate and continue to practice peaceful coexistence."[13]

This is not a modern phenomenon. The Copts are the indigenous people of Egypt and number as many as 20 million around the world. They are one of the most ancient Christian groups in the world and maintain the practices of the earliest Christians. Consequently they have been the victims of centuries of violence and oppression, chiefly in Egypt, for practicing their Christian faith. They are the first religious group ever to have been nominated for the Nobel Peace Prize.

Jesus says that one must expect persecution if one follows his way of spirituality. Indeed he said, "Whoever wants to be my disciple must deny themselves and take up their cross and follow me." (Matthew 16:24) Suffering, and even death, are the consequence of following Jesus. Indeed persecution can even be seen as a barometer of faithfulness to the way of Jesus. If people hate you, then you must be doing something right. As Winston Churchill said, "You have enemies? Good. That means you've stood up for something, sometime in your life." That is what Jesus is saying. He pronounces a blessing on the persecuted. "Blessed are those who are persecuted for righteousness' sake, for theirs is the kingdom of heaven."

Then Jesus does something he has not done in any of the other beatitudes. He addresses the hearer directly in a ninth blessing. "Blessed are you when others revile you and persecute you and utter all kinds of evil against you falsely on my account. Rejoice and be glad, for your reward is great in heaven, for so they persecuted the prophets who were before you." (Matthew 5:10-12) This is not a general benediction which applies to anyone. Jesus is speaking directly to the listener. He makes it personal and draws us in. He challenges us to follow the road less traveled.

There are prophets, and there is the crowd. There are those who walk the narrow way, and those who travel the highway of the masses. Jesus calls his followers to take the prophetic path in all they say and do. If we do, we can be sure to receive the prophet's reward – both the bad and the good. "Whoever receives you receives me, and whoever receives me receives him who sent me. The one who receives a prophet because he is a prophet will receive a prophet's reward, and the one who receives a righteous person because he is a righteous person will receive a righteous person's reward. And whoever gives one of these little ones even a cup of cold water because he is a disciple, truly, I say to you, he will by no means lose his reward." (Matthew 10:40-42)

The fact that Jesus blesses those whom the world curses points to a different way of understanding suffering. One can see beyond the immediacy of the situation to a higher spiritual reality. Suffering is put in a bigger context. This in turn means that one can face suffering with a greater degree of acceptance, knowing that it is unavoidable in the spiritual life. Suffering is not a sign of divine displeasure or indifference. Neither is it an evil to be avoided or overcome. Suffering is part of the spiritual life. The suffering of persecution is a sign that one is on the right path – the way of the cross.

To end the beatitudes Jesus adds a tenth statement, making his beatitudes a clear parallel to Moses' Ten Commandments. Jesus says, "Rejoice and be glad, for your reward is great in heaven, for so they persecuted the prophets who were before you." (Matthew 5:10-12) This is the only command among the beatitudes. But it is not a moralistic "thou shalt not." It is a call to "rejoice and be glad" even in terrible circumstances.

How different are Jesus' beatitudes than Moses' list of commands! This is the difference between religion and spirituality. Instead of a list of divine injunctions with consequences of rewards and punishments, Jesus blesses those in the most difficult circumstances. The only command among them is a command to rejoice and be glad no matter what! It is reminiscent of Paul's command to "give thanks in all circumstances; for this is God's will for you in Christ Jesus." (I Thessalonians 5:18) The way of Jesus is a way of blessing. It is a way of joy. It is the way of true spirituality, which both transcends and fulfils the way of human religion.

Self-Knowledge

The beatitudes serve as an introduction to the Sermon on the Mount. After the beatitudes the sermon begins in earnest. Jesus' sermon can be entitled "True Spirituality." True spirituality begins with a correct understanding of self. Our understanding of who we are is the foundation of everything else. If we don't know who – or what – we are, we cannot know where we come from or where we are going. Nor can we know the meaning and purpose of life.

"Know thyself" was the Greek inscription that greeted ancient pilgrims at the entrance to the temple at Delphi. Self-knowledge is the beginning of the spiritual search. Before one can seek God, one must know who is seeking God. When one knows oneself, everything else becomes clearer. Discovery of our true nature opens our eyes to the nature of God and the world.

The psalmist mused, "What is man that thou art mindful of him?" (Psalm 8:4) Historically, the answer given to that question by orthodox Christianity has been that humans are physical creatures made by a divine Creator. We are beings made in the image of God composed of a mortal body and an immortal soul. (This body-soul dualism, by the way, came from Greek philosophy and not from Scripture. It was baptized into Christianity very early in the history of the Church.)

According to the Church humans were created good, but willfully fell into sin through disobedience. We are fallen creatures deserving of eternal punishment from a holy and just Deity. We are "sinners in the hands of an angry God," as Jonathan Edwards described the human predicament in his famous sermon. We are lost souls in need of redemption. According to orthodox Christian theology, salvation is achieved through a blood sacrifice, which was provided by Jesus Christ on the cross.

Jesus never mentions any of this in his teachings. This is a later Christian understanding of Jesus' death as interpreted in the light of the Old Testament sacrificial system. What does Jesus say about human identity? He uses two metaphors. He says, "You are salt" and "You are light."

First he uses the metaphor of salt. "You are the salt of the earth, but if salt has lost its taste, how shall its saltiness be restored? It is no longer good for anything except to be thrown out and trampled under people's feet." (Matthew 5:13)

Jesus was not the first spiritual teacher to use the metaphor of salt to describe our essential nature. The Upanishads use the same metaphor as part of the teaching of a father to a son, a literary technique also used in the Old Testament Book of Proverbs.

"Please, Father, tell me more about this Self."
"Yes, dear one, I will," Uddalaka said.
"Place this salt in water and bring it here
    tomorrow morning." The boy did.
"Where is that salt?" his father asked. "I do
    not see it."
"Sip here. How does it taste?"
"Salty, Father."
"And here? And there?"
"I taste salt everywhere."
"It is everywhere, though we see it not.
Just so, dear one, the Self is everywhere,
Within all things, although we see him not.
There is nothing that does not come from
    him.
Of everything he is the inmost Self.
He is the truth; he is the Self supreme.
You are that, Shvetaketu; you are that."[14]

Jesus said, "You are the salt of the earth." It is common for Christian interpreters to wax eloquent about salt's healing and preservative properties and its monetary value in the ancient world. But that is not what Jesus talks about. To focus on those extraneous properties of salt is to miss Jesus' point. He specifically mentions the taste of salt, and says that without saltiness, salt has no meaning or purpose. Then it is no longer salt, and it is discarded as worthless. The nature and purpose of salt is to become part of food or drink, where it is invisible yet undeniably present.

A person's true nature is like salt. If we remain separate we are "good for nothing" to use Jesus' words. Our true nature is indistinguishable from the cosmos, like salt permeating food or water. We live only when we die to ourselves, as Jesus says elsewhere. (Matthew 16:24–25; Mark 8:34–35) If we seek to save our lives then we are lost. Only when we let go of our selves, do we gain eternal life.

Jesus also uses the metaphor of light. "You are the light of the world. A city set on a hill cannot be hidden. Nor do people light a lamp and put it under a basket, but on a stand, and it gives light to all in the house. In the same way, let your light shine before others, so that they may see your good works and give glory to your Father who is in heaven." (Matthew 5:14-16)

Our true nature is like light. Christian preachers tend to explore all the characteristics of light, but Jesus focuses on only two aspects. They are the same two points he makes about salt. Those two qualities are nonlocality and functionality. Salt permeates water and food. It is not localized. Furthermore its function is to provide taste. Likewise light is nonlocal. It is everywhere. It is not confined to the city or the lamp. It shines forth from the city and spreads throughout the house. Its function is to illuminate everything around it.

Light – like dissolved salt - is invisible. But it illuminates the world. We are the light of the world. We are the salt of the earth. The essential nature of salt and light are their invisible and permeable presence. As the Gospel of Thomas (113) says, "The Kingdom of the Father is spread out upon the earth, and men do not see it." This is how Jesus describes the Kingdom of God in the canonical gospels. "The Kingdom of God is in your midst," he said. It is also translated "within you." (Luke 17:21) It is both. In both the metaphors of salt and light Jesus is describing our essential nature as nonlocal and functional.

Jesus says in the Gospel of Thomas, "If those who lead you say, 'See, the Kingdom is in the sky,' then the birds of the sky will precede you. If they say to you, 'It is in the sea,' then the fish will precede you. Rather, the Kingdom is inside of you, and it is outside of you. When you come to know yourselves, then you will become known, and you will realize that it is you who are the sons of the living Father. But if you will not know yourselves, you dwell in poverty and it is you who are that poverty." (Thomas 3)

We are more than physical creatures in a physical universe. We are not just individuals who live a few decades and return to the dust from which we came. Neither are we separate souls located in physical bodies. Our essential nature is neither individual nor local. We are part of the cosmos. Our nature is universal and pervasive. Our true nature permeates the world like salt permeates water and like light permeates air.

Furthermore we have function and purpose in the universe. Jesus says, "In the same way, let your light shine before others, so that they may see your good works and give glory to your Father who is in heaven." Our function is who we are. We are more like verbs than nouns. We are more a process than entities. Salt flavors and light illuminates. We flavor and illuminate the universe.

As you read these words, please remember that this is not a theological concept. It is not a doctrine. I am not advocating a philosophical idea, which can be dismissed by labelling it pantheism or monism. Jesus was not a theologian or a philosopher. Neither am I. These are metaphors and analogies. These images of salt and light are meant to point to something which cannot be communicated through theology or doctrine. To reduce this teaching to an idea is to misunderstand it. He was communicating the experiential reality of Christian spirituality, not a metaphysical concept.

Our essential nature can be experienced, but it cannot be described. It can be known intimately and intuitively, but not intellectually.

"Know thyself" is not a command to believe a particular theory of human origins or a "doctrine of man." It is an invitation to become aware of who we are through direct experience. This truth is found in the teaching of Jesus and other spiritual traditions. We are the salt of the earth. We are the light of the world.

Spirituality

Jesus did not have a good relationship with the religion of his day. When he preached in his hometown synagogue of Nazareth, they kicked him out of the building. Later Jesus returned the favor. Jesus took a whip of cords and drove the moneychangers out of the temple courts and overturned their booths. He said, "It is written, My house will be a house of prayer, but you have made it a den of thieves!" (Luke 19:46)

He called the scribes and Pharisees "hypocrites" and every other name imaginable, including children of the devil (John 8:44). Matthew 23 has a long list of "woes" spoken by Jesus against the teachers of the law and the Pharisees, detailing how they had turned religion into something evil. The religious authorities did not tolerate Jesus' outspoken criticism for very long. When given the opportunity, they had him arrested and executed.

Jesus did not love religion, and it did not love him back. Therefore it is ironic that a religion grew up around him after his death, complete with priests and rituals and its own hypocrisy. Jesus advocated a spirituality that transcended religion. The "spiritual but not religious" people of today would have felt at home with him.

Yet Jesus was not anti-religion. He certainly was not anti-scripture. He just hated how religious people corrupted religion and scripture. He wanted to return to the essence of true religion. He wanted to fulfil the meaning and purpose of the scriptures of his childhood faith.

Jesus said, "Do not think that I have come to abolish the Law or the Prophets; I have not come to abolish them but to fulfill them. For truly, I say to you, until heaven and earth pass away, not an iota, not a dot, will pass from the Law until all is accomplished. Therefore whoever relaxes one of the least of these commandments and teaches others to do the same will be called least in the kingdom of heaven, but whoever does them and teaches them will be called great in the kingdom of heaven. For I tell you, unless your righteousness exceeds that of the scribes and Pharisees, you will never enter the kingdom of heaven." (Matthew 5:17-20)

Jesus advocated and practiced spirituality without religion, not unlike the "religionless Christianity" described by Dietrich Bonhoeffer. While imprisoned by the Nazis, German pastor and theologian Dietrich Bonhoeffer wrote several letters from Tegel prison to his friend Eberhard Bethge. In them he spoke of the need for a "religionless Christianity." In a note dated November 21, 1943, he wrote, "I shall not come out of here a homo religiosus! My fear and distrust of 'religiosity' have become greater than ever here."

On April 30, 1944, Bonhoeffer wrote, "What is bothering me incessantly is the question what Christianity really is, or indeed who Christ really is, for us today." He continues, "Are there religionless Christians? If religion is only a garment of Christianity — and even this garment has looked very different at different times — then what is a religionless Christianity?"

He says, "We are moving towards a completely religionless time; people as they are now simply cannot be religious anymore. Even those who honestly describe themselves as 'religious' do not in the least act up to it, and so they presumably mean something quite different by 'religious'... And if therefore man becomes radically religionless — and I think that is already more or less the case (else, how is it, for example, that this war, in contrast to all previous ones, is not calling forth any 'religious' reaction?) — what does that mean for 'Christianity'?"[15]

The backdrop of Bonhoeffer's words was a German Evangelical Church which had surrendered to Nazi control, willingly accepting a bishop appointed by the Third Reich. He watched as Christians looked the other way while evils were committed by the state. Christianity had proven itself to be morally bankrupt. Preachers turned their backs on their responsibility to be a prophetic voice in society and had become chaplains for a national political leader.

Bonhoeffer's words remind me of the times we live in today in America. The majority of Christians have turned their backs on the Kingdom of God in order to endorse a worldly political and religious system. Woody Allen's line in his film *Hannah and Her Sisters* echoes my own visceral reaction to our current situation: "If Jesus came back and saw what's going on in his name, He'd never stop throwing up."

American Christianity has lost its spiritual and moral compass. It has sold its soul to a political party in order to advance a social agenda that has no basis in scripture. Christianity has abandoned God and the Scriptures. In the words of Jesus, "Woe to you, teachers of the law and Pharisees, you hypocrites! You travel over land and sea to win a single convert, and when you have succeeded, you make them twice as much a child of hell as you are." (Matthew 23:15) In such a moral and spiritual climate, the only option for a spiritually-minded person is to adopt a "religionless Christianity." That is what Jesus was doing in his time.

Today there is a movement called "Red Letter Christians" who are trying to return Christianity to its roots in the teachings of Jesus. It gets its name from versions of the New Testament that print the words of Jesus in red ink. It takes the Sermon on the Mount as the norm for Christian ethics and seeks to be a prophetic voice in a society and a religion which has lost its way. If Jesus came back and saw what they were doing, he would respond, "Well done, good and faithful servants."

Forgiveness

Forgiveness is the mark of a Christian. At least it should be. Christian theology is predicated on the belief that we have been forgiven of our sins by God through Jesus Christ. Having experienced such mercy in our lives, we therefore have the power to be able to forgive others. Unforgiveness in our lives indicates that we have not experienced divine forgiveness.

According to Jesus, violence in the world can be traced back to unforgiveness in the heart. He said:

> You have heard that it was said to those of old, 'You shall not murder; and whoever murders will be liable to judgment.' But I say to you that everyone who is angry with his brother will be liable to judgment; whoever insults his brother will be liable to the council; and whoever says, 'You fool!' will be liable to the hell of fire. So if you are offering your gift at the altar and there remember that your brother has something against you, leave your gift there before the altar and go. First be reconciled to your brother, and then come and offer your gift. Come to terms

quickly with your accuser while you are going with him to court, lest your accuser hand you over to the judge, and the judge to the guard, and you be put in prison. Truly, I say to you, you will never get out until you have paid the last penny. (Matthew 5:21-26)

The Ten Commandments say, "You shall not murder." Murder has consequences in the Old Testament law. It is known as lex talionis, or the law of retaliation. The principle says that a person who has injured another is to be penalized to a similar degree. In the Bible it is exemplified by the phrases "an eye for an eye" and "a tooth for a tooth." It finds its ultimate expression in capital punishment.

As Jesus often does in the Sermon on the Mount, he exhorts his followers to transcend the moral laws of religion and society. Instead of focusing on the external command not to murder, Jesus goes deeper into the inner motivation for murder. The problem of killing begins in the heart. It is a problem of anger. He says that anger is manifested not only in physical attacks, but verbal attacks. To insult someone or call them a fool is enough to send a person to hell in Jesus' view.

When we ponder Jesus' words, it makes us stop focusing on the sins of other people, and causes us to look at our own sin. Religion is concerned with external behavior, and for that reason is prone to hypocrisy. On the other hand, the spirituality of Jesus is concerned mainly with one's internal spiritual condition.

Religion looks at other people and judges – often harshly. Spirituality is introspective; it looks at oneself and particularly into one's own heart. Religion issues condemnations of others for offenses they have committed. Spirituality produces humility. By Jesus' standards we are no better than anyone else. As God said to Samuel, "Man looks on the outward appearance, but the Lord looks on the heart." (I Samuel 16:7)

The only difference between a murderer sitting on death row and us sitting in a pew is that we have not acted on our impulses. That is likely due more to the external circumstances of our lives than any inner moral restraint. That could be us laying on the ground with 16 bullets pumped into our body by the police. That could be us holding the gun. "There but for the grace of God, go I." The realization that internally we are no different than a murderer prompts an attitude of introspection, which in turn elicits forgiveness and reconciliation toward those who have sinned against us.

It should also prompt us to revamp our criminal justice system – to transform it from retributive justice to restorative and rehabilitative justice. The reason a person commits a crime has as much to do with the environment that a person lives in (and was raised in) as it does with his morality. If we desire to build a just, safe, and compassionate society, then we must look beyond the act committed to the origins of that act in a person's soul and in our society.

On a purely personal and individual level, forgiveness is the healthiest option for a person who is serious about the spiritual life. The apostle Paul, who had more than enough reasons to hold a grudge, said, "Repay no one evil for evil, but give thought to do what is honorable in the sight of all. If possible, so far as it depends on you, live peaceably with all. Beloved, never avenge yourselves, but leave it to the wrath of God, for it is written, 'Vengeance is mine, I will repay, says the Lord.' To the contrary, 'if your enemy is hungry, feed him; if he is thirsty, give him something to drink; for by so doing you will heap burning coals on his head.' Do not be overcome by evil, but overcome evil with good." (Romans 12:17-21)

I do not like Paul's insinuation that God will personally take the revenge that we refuse to take. I think that is unworthy of a forgiving and loving God. But I appreciate the apostle's willingness to forgo vengeance in his personal life. Indeed he encourages readers to act contrary to their natural retaliatory instincts. I suspect this is a way to internally counteract the tendency to hold grudges even if we forsake revenge. His comment about "heaping burning coals on his head" betrays the conflicting emotions in Paul's own heart. But in the end he comes out in the right place. He instructs us not let evil win, but to overcome evil with good.

Unforgiveness is a spiritual poison which causes more harm to us than to those who have harmed us. It will hinder our spiritual growth more certainly than anything else. It is a cancer that eats at our soul until our inner life is withered and dead. The only cure for anger and resentment is the unconditional love of God experienced and demonstrated in our lives. Such love is not the natural state of the human heart. It must be cultivated through introspection and discipline. As the apostle of love writes:

> So we have come to know and to believe the love that God has for us. God is love, and whoever abides in love abides in God, and God abides in him. By this is love perfected with us.... There is no fear in love, but perfect love casts out fear. For fear has to do with punishment, and whoever fears has not been perfected in love. We love because he first loved us. If anyone says, "I love God," and hates his brother, he is a liar; for he who does not love his brother whom he has seen cannot love God whom he has not seen. And this commandment we have from him: whoever loves God must also love his brother. (I John 4:16-21)

Sexual Integrity

Jesus talked about sex. He did not talk much about it. Not nearly as much as Christians do today. For example, he does not mention homosexuality, even though the Old Testament does and the apostle Paul does. It was certainly known in his day, yet Jesus fails to address the subject. Why he did not talk about the matter is open for debate. But in any case he did not deem it important enough to include in his inaugural sermon.

On the other hand, heterosexual sin was very much on his mind. He focuses on adultery. Jesus said, "You have heard that it was said, 'You shall not commit adultery.' But I say to you that everyone who looks at a woman with lustful intent has already committed adultery with her in his heart." (Matthew 5:27-28) Once again Jesus stresses the internal rather than the external nature of sin. According to Jesus the real problem is lust, not sex.

Spirituality is more a matter of the heart than actions. If the heart is right, then the actions that flow from the heart will be right. If the heart is wrong, what flows from it will be wrong. As Jesus says, "For no good tree bears bad fruit, nor again does a bad tree bear good fruit, for each tree is known by its own fruit. For figs are not gathered from thornbushes, nor are grapes picked from a bramble bush. The good person out of the good treasure of his heart produces good, and the evil person out of his evil treasure produces evil, for out of the abundance of the heart his mouth speaks." (Luke 6:43-45)

Sexual morality is a matter of the heart. If the heart is right, then the sexual expressions that flow from it are right. If the heart is wrong then the sexual acts that flow from it are wrong. Jesus' thoughts on sex were entirely related to the violation of marriage. He never talks about sex by unmarried persons. Premarital sex, which consumes so much of Christian morality, is never addressed by Jesus.

Some commentators would disagree with me on this point. They would point to Jesus's use of the word porneia (πορνεία), often translated as "sexual immorality" or "fornication." But one has to read such an interpretation into his use of the word. It is not contained in the context of the gospels. His use of the word in the Sermon on the Mount is clearly referring to adultery committed by married persons and not sex by unmarried persons.

Jesus is concerned about the preservation of marriage. Adultery is a violation of the marriage vows. Divorce is a violation of the marriage covenant. Jesus quotes the Old Testament regulation which permitted divorce and holds his followers to a higher standard. "It was also said, 'Whoever divorces his wife, let him give her a certificate of divorce.' But I say to you that everyone who divorces his wife, except on the ground of sexual immorality, makes her commit adultery, and whoever marries a divorced woman commits adultery. Matthew 5:31-32)

The exception clause "except on the ground of sexual immorality" was likely added to Jesus' words by a later scribe. Parallel passages in the earlier Gospel of Mark and also in the later Gospel of Luke include no exception cause. It is probable that a later copyist inserted this loophole into the Sermon on the Mount. It goes against the spirit of Jesus' spirituality and smacks of legalism. The copyist saw Jesus' words as a new law rather than as a teaching that transcended the legalistic mindset.

Jesus was concerned, as always, with the heart. Religion obsesses over actions. It seems to be especially interested in actions done in the bedroom. Spirituality looks at the intentions of the heart. Deeds are the overflow of the heart. Get the heart right and the actions cannot be wrong.

Augustine said, "Love, and do what you will." It is a good rule to live by when understood correctly. Augustine's words can be misinterpreted to advocate lawlessness.

Therefore this influential 4th and 5th century theologian expounds on his saying.

> See what we are insisting upon; that the deeds of men are only discerned by the root of charity. For many things may be done that have a good appearance, and yet proceed not from the root of charity. For thorns also have flowers: some actions truly seem rough, seem savage; howbeit they are done for discipline at the bidding of charity. Once for all, then, a short precept is given you: Love, and do what you will: whether you hold your peace, through love hold your peace; whether you cry out, through love cry out; whether you correct, through love correct; whether you spare, through love do you spare: let the root of love be within, of this root can nothing spring but what is good.[16]

Jesus understood sexuality as a matter of the heart. The morality of sexual acts depends on the intentions. Love is Jesus' guiding principle in this matter, as in all matters. As Jesus says elsewhere, the whole law can be summed up in two commands: Love God and love your neighbor. To paraphrase the apostle Paul in Romans 14:23, anything that is not of love is sin. Conversely anything that stems from love cannot be sin.

Truthfulness

The goal of the spiritual life is truth in all its fullness. "Truth, the whole truth and nothing but the truth." All truth is God's truth. This means that truth arrived at through a rigorous scientific method is God's truth. It means that one's spiritual worldview must incorporate the latest scientific discoveries. For example, young earth creationism, which does not acknowledge that the universe is billions of years old and that life on earth evolved over millions of years, is based on a lie.

Truth is iconoclastic. It tears down the idols and false gods of religion, including the idols of Christianity. When one searches one's own spiritual tradition - as well as the spiritual traditions of the world – looking for truth, one must be relentless in exposing falsehood. The God of Truth is a jealous God. "You shall have no other gods before me." Mythological interpretations of reality that have hardened into literalistic dogma must be discarded in the name of the God of Truth. Beliefs must make way for truth.

Truth is not just a matter of worldview. It is a concern of the soul. We are self-deceptive creatures. We propagate falsehoods about ourselves and others to buttress our public persona, which we have carefully constructed as the face we present to the world. We edit our personal history and our collective histories to create a version of reality in keeping with our latest understanding of who we are. As Supreme Court nominee Brett Kavanaugh said under oath in refuting the accusations of sexual assault made against him, "That is not who I am. That is not who I was."

It has been scientifically demonstrated that memories are selective at best. At worst they are unreliable. Memories are not like digital recordings stored in the brain, which can be accessed at will. Memories are malleable and constantly changing as our self-image changes. We are continually editing our personal autobiographies to conform to our newest understanding of ourselves.

We do this as cultures as well as individuals. Eliot Peper writes, "Like memory, history was synthetic. Humans thought of both as factual records, but study after study confirmed that they were more like dreams, narratives constructed and reconstructed by the mind to fit the demands of the present, not the reality of the past."[17]

We habitually lie to ourselves and others. To counteract this tendency, societies and religions have created mechanisms to ensure we tell the truth. It enforces truth-telling by meting out appropriate punishments if we are found to lie under oath. We "swear to God," "swear on the Bible," and even "swear on my mother's grave" that we are telling the truth. But none of this matters if we believe our own lies. Jesus does away with the religious practice of oaths. He says:

> Again you have heard that it was said to those of old, 'You shall not swear falsely, but shall perform to the Lord what you have sworn.' But I say to you, Do not take an oath at all, either by heaven, for it is the throne of God, or by the earth, for it is his footstool, or by Jerusalem, for it is the city of the great King. And do not take an oath by your head, for you cannot make one hair white or black. Let what you say be simply 'Yes' or 'No'; anything more than this comes from evil. (Matthew 5:33-37)

Jesus calls us to transparency. The spiritual life cannot thrive in the toxic atmosphere of deceit – especially self-deceit. The fictions of our lives are to be set aside in the search for truth. We are to be brutally honest with ourselves if we are to come to the place of spiritual Truth.

In practice this means that we are to maintain an attitude of skepticism toward those who say they have the truth. We are to question authority, especially religious authority, whether that comes in the form of infallible popes, authoritative creeds, or inerrant scriptures. Jesus' Sermon on the Mount is an assault on traditional interpretation of scripture. He repeatedly says, "You have heard that it was said ... but I say to you...." At the end of the sermon the gospel writer says that the people who heard Jesus marveled because he spoke with authority and not as one of their scribes. (Matthew 7:28-29)

Unfortunately American spirituality is populated by the gullible, who will believe anything that their religious authorities tell them. The fact that so many people can believe incredible and nonsensical things in the name of religion should cause us to second-guess our own ability to discern truth from falsehood when it comes to spiritual matters. Are we really so different than Mormons, who believe that Native Americans are the descendants of the lost tribes of Israel, or Scientologists, who believe humans came from space aliens?

In the spiritual life, truth is all that matters. We must question anyone who says we must take things "on faith." We are to seek truth, love truth, and speak truth. We are to embody truth in our lives. We are to live truthfully and transparently in accord with the highest truth we know, regardless of the consequences. Life is too short to play spiritual games. We must be ruthless in our rejection of falsehood, especially when it resides in our own religious tradition. As much as we can avoid the trap of self-deceit, let us live and speak truth.

Generosity

In the spiritual life there is a continual battle between the self and the Self, the ego and the Spirit. The ego wants recognition. It wants to be acknowledged as "spiritual." It yearns to possess eternal life in the form of never-ending existence of the ego. Its God is made in its own image - a Superego in heaven who reigns over all. It wants every knee to bow and every tongue confess how wonderful it is. It is insecure and wants ceaseless worship and praise. It wants to be recognized for being holy and good.

The Spirit is just the opposite. It does not seek the limelight. Like water it seeks the lowest place. It empties itself, takes the form of a servant, and dies to self. That is the meaning of the cross. (Philippians 2:5-8) Only when the ego dies, does the Spirit live. Jesus says in the Gospel of John, "Truly, truly, I say to you, unless a grain of wheat falls into the earth and dies, it remains alone; but if it dies, it bears much fruit. Whoever loves his life loses it, and whoever hates his life in this world will keep it for eternal life." (John 12:24-25)

When one walks the way of Jesus, one gives of oneself and one's resources, without thought of recognition or reward. Giving is done naturally and unselfconsciously, like the sun giving light. Jesus says, "Beware of practicing your righteousness before other people in order to be seen by them, for then you will have no reward from your Father who is in heaven. Thus, when you give to the needy, sound no trumpet before you, as the hypocrites do in the synagogues and in the streets, that they may be praised by others. Truly, I say to you, they have received their reward. But when you give to the needy, do not let your left hand know what your right hand is doing, so that your giving may be in secret. And your Father who sees in secret will reward you. (Matthew 6:1-4)

To illustrate his point Jesus points his disciples to a poor widow putting her alms into the temple treasury. "Jesus looked up and saw the rich putting their gifts into the offering box, and he saw a poor widow put in two small copper coins. And he said, 'Truly, I tell you, this poor widow has put in more than all of them. For they all contributed out of their abundance, but she out of her poverty put in all she had to live on.'" (Luke 21:1-4) The woman gave unselfconsciously, one might say she gave recklessly. She did not calculate her tithe carefully to be sure she had enough left for herself. She gave with no thought to the morrow. (Matthew 6:34)

That is the nature of the spiritual life. The egoic self takes a backseat. In the highest form of the spiritual life, the self no longer lives, but is entirely surrendered to the Spirit, who works through the vestigial structure of the human self, serving the Divine purpose without awareness of the cost. As Paul says, "It is no longer I who live, but Christ who lives in me." (Galatians 2:20)

Nonviolence

It is clear to anyone who has read the Gospels that Jesus preached nonviolence. Furthermore he practiced what he preached. It is also clear that the church that bears his name today does not preach or practice his ethic of nonviolence. Christianity – especially its more conservative American forms – endorses guns and military strength.

This is a glaring indication that the Christian religion has forsaken the spirituality of Jesus. It is to our shame that the first person in modern times to take Jesus' ethic seriously and put it into practice as a social force was a Hindu. He was Mohandas Gandhi, known as Mahatma, "the great soul." His practice of ahimsa, the principle of nonviolence toward all living things, came as much from Jesus as his Hindu religion.

When asked why he did not become a Christian, since he loved the Sermon on the Mount so much, he responded, "I would become a Christian, if I ever met one." When a Baptist preacher named Martin King looked for an example of Christian nonviolence to combat the racism of white Christian Southerners, he had to learn the ethic of Jesus, not from his seminary professors, from this Indian sage.

Jesus said, "You have heard that it was said, 'An eye for an eye and a tooth for a tooth.' But I say to you, Do not resist the one who is evil. But if anyone slaps you on the right cheek, turn to him the other also. And if anyone would sue you and take your tunic, let him have your cloak as well. And if anyone forces you to go one mile, go with him two miles. Give to the one who begs from you, and do not refuse the one who would borrow from you." (Matthew 5:38-42)

Jesus quotes the religious law from the Torah and directly refutes it. He challenges his followers to take the higher road. It is not just a matter of legalistically refusing to use physical force. It is deeper and broader than that. Jesus rejects legal retaliation. If someone sues you, give him more than he asks. How would that work in our litigious society, where Christians band together to demand their rights, and routinely take their enemies to court? Christians even take each other to court! Paul addresses this situation in his letter to the Corinthian Christians. "To have lawsuits at all with one another is already a defeat for you. Why not rather suffer wrong? Why not rather be defrauded?" (I Corinthians 6:7)

Jesus makes reference to the right under Roman law of occupying Roman soldiers to force Jews to carry their packs up to one mile. Jesus tells his followers to willingly carry it twice as far as they are required. What would happen if Palestinian Christians practiced this against their Israeli oppressors today? Jesus is not advocating acquiescence to oppression. But he is teaching us to cultivate an inner attitude of nonresistance, which is the root of the practice of nonviolence. Once again Jesus is more concerned with the inner than the outer. He goes on to talk about love of enemy.

Jesus says, "You have heard that it was said, 'You shall love your neighbor and hate your enemy.' But I say to you, Love your enemies and pray for those who persecute you, so that you may be sons of your Father who is in heaven. For he makes his sun rise on the evil and on the good, and sends rain on the just and on the unjust. For if you love those who love you, what reward do you have? Do not even the tax collectors do the same? And if you greet only your brothers, what more are you doing than others? Do not even the Gentiles do the same? You therefore must be perfect, as your heavenly Father is perfect." (Matthew 5:43-48)

I am writing these words in the midst of the 2018 midterm election campaign. I have never witnessed such hate between members of opposing parties. The ones who appear to hate the most – at least they are the most vocal and loudest – are the ones who profess to be Christians! It just shows how far Christianity has fallen from its origins. Have they never read the words of their Savior? Why is it that Christians so easy fall into hatemongering? I can only conclude that they are only Christian in an outward religious sense and not an inner spiritual sense.

Jesus calls us to love our enemies. This is not a lofty ideal to work toward. This is a practical ethic for everyday life. Those who claim to follow Jesus are to be different than those who do not know Jesus. We are to love not only those who love us, agree with us, and share our social values and political agenda. If we love only those who are on our side, how are we different than the world? Even though the apostle Paul never met Jesus or heard him preach, he shared this same ethic of nonviolence. He writes:

> Let love be genuine. Abhor what is evil; hold fast to what is good. Love one another with brotherly affection. Outdo one another in showing honor. Do not be slothful in zeal, be fervent in spirit, serve the Lord. Rejoice in hope, be patient in tribulation, be constant in prayer. Contribute to the needs of the saints and seek to show hospitality. Bless those who persecute you; bless and do not curse them. Rejoice with those who rejoice, weep with those who weep. Live in harmony with one another. Do not be haughty, but associate with the lowly. Never be wise in your own sight. Repay no one evil for evil, but give thought to do what is honorable in the sight of all. If possible, so far as it depends on you,

live peaceably with all.... Do not be overcome by evil, but overcome evil with good. (Rom 12:9-21)

This ethic of nonviolence is probably the one area where Christians could be the most noticeably different from other people in American society... if only we would heed the words of Jesus. How extraordinary would it be if all Christians practiced the Sermon on the Mount!

Prayer

The most distinguishable practice of the religious life is prayer. Like all other spiritual practices, prayer is open to abuse. It can be practiced in a self-serving manner to enhance one's standing and reputation in the community rather than as a form of personal connection to God. Therefore Jesus gives a lengthy instruction on how to pray.

> And when you pray, you must not be like the hypocrites. For they love to stand and pray in the synagogues and at the street corners, that they may be seen by others. Truly, I say to you, they have received their reward. But when you pray, go into your room and shut the door and pray to your Father who is in secret. And your Father who sees in secret will reward you.

> And when you pray, do not heap up empty phrases as the Gentiles do, for they think that they will be heard for their many words. Do not be like them, for your Father knows what you need before you ask him. Pray then like this: "Our Father in heaven, hallowed be your name. Your

kingdom come, your will be done, on earth as it is in heaven. Give us this day our daily bread, and forgive us our debts, as we also have forgiven our debtors. And lead us not into temptation, but deliver us from evil. For if you forgive others their trespasses, your heavenly Father will also forgive you, but if you do not forgive others their trespasses, neither will your Father forgive your trespasses.

And when you fast, do not look gloomy like the hypocrites, for they disfigure their faces that their fasting may be seen by others. Truly, I say to you, they have received their reward. But when you fast, anoint your head and wash your face, that your fasting may not be seen by others but by your Father who is in secret. And your Father who sees in secret will reward you. (Matthew 6:5-18)

Jesus mentions four qualities of genuine prayer. First it is private. John Wooden said, "The true test of a man's character is what he does when no one is watching." That is certainly true when it comes to prayer. Public prayer is susceptible to all sorts of baser motives. But when one is alone with God with the door closed, then one's true relationship to God is exposed. There is no hiding from God or one's own soul. Only in solitude can true prayer happen. The same is true of spiritual disciplines such as fasting, which Jesus mentions specifically. In the spiritual life one can opt for the outward reward or the inward one.

The second quality is brevity. In my career as a minister I have heard some very long prayers prayed by laypeople and clergy. They are almost always unnecessary. If the person who prays really believes that God knows what we need before we ask, then why the long prayers? Why the flowery language? Prayer cannot inform God of anything God does not already know. Its purpose is to get our requests out into the open where we can acknowledge our needs and wants. Once the concerns of our heart are brought into the light, then the work of prayer is done.

To that end Jesus offers a model prayer, known today as the Lord's Prayer. It was likely not intended to be recited – and certainly not intoned mindlessly – but meant to be an example of what one should mention in prayer. In this prayer Jesus emphasizes a third quality of genuine prayer – forgiveness. If we ask for forgiveness from God, then we must be willing to forgive. Jesus seems to imply that we are forgiven only to the extent that we forgive. This is certainly a motivation for unconditional forgiveness!

The fourth quality of prayer is persistence, which Jesus mentions a little later in the Sermon on the Mount. "Keep on asking, and you will receive what you ask for. Keep on seeking, and you will find. Keep on knocking, and the door will be opened to you. For everyone who asks, receives. Everyone who seeks, finds. And to everyone who knocks, the door will be opened. You parents — if your children ask for a loaf of bread, do you give them a stone instead? Or if they ask for a fish, do you give them a snake? Of course not! So if you sinful people know how to give good gifts to your children, how much more will your heavenly Father give good gifts to those who ask him." (7:7-11 New Living Translation)

Prayer, like all spiritual disciplines, are to be practiced consistently over the long term. Expect no immediate results. Nothing worthwhile comes quickly or easily. Modern offers of shortcuts to enlightenment or instant salvation should be treated warily. As the old saying goes, "if it sounds too good to be true, it probably is." Prayer takes time and practice. It takes a lifetime of discipline to mature in the practice of prayer. In a certain sense one remains a beginner all one's life. Expect to make mistakes. Expect there to be failures. That is how we learn. That is why it is called "practice."

Simplicity

In the nineteenth century Alexis de Tocqueville observed of Americans: "I know of no country where the love of money has taken stronger hold on the affections of men. Love of money is either the chief or secondary motive in everything Americans do." This is even truer in the twenty-first century. The desire for material possessions has infiltrated – and in some areas come to dominate – the American church.

Christianity today is plagued by a form of religious idolatry known as the Prosperity Gospel, also called the Health and Wealth Gospel, or the Gospel of Success. This "prosperity theology" teaches that financial wealth is the will of God for Christians. One receives this blessing through faith, positive thinking, and by giving financial donations to Christian ministries. The largest church in the United States, the Lakewood Church in Houston, Texas, led by charismatic pastor Joel Osteen, teaches this gospel.

Many other churches follow their lead, hoping for similar success. A 2018 survey by LifeWay Research found that 38 percent of Protestant churchgoers agree with the statement, "My church teaches that if I give more money to my church and charities, God will bless me in return."[18] Even the "mom and pop" churches in small towns focus an inordinate amount of time on church finances and physical property. "Success" is measured by the church's financial status and buildings.

Jesus would not recognize such an attitude as having anything to do with his gospel. For Jesus the poor and the "poor in spirit" are the ones who are blessed by God. "Theirs is the Kingdom of Heaven." Jesus had no use for money or buildings. In his only violent act recorded in the New Testament, Jesus made a whip of cords and drove the money changers out of the temple. He prophesied that God would execute his judgement on the gold-encrusted Jerusalem temple by destroying it completely.

Jesus would have agreed with the Pastoral epistle that says, "The love of money is the root of all kinds of evil." (I Timothy 6:10) Jesus confessed that he owned nothing. He had no place to lay his head, and he called his followers to follow his example. He called his disciples to drop everything – to leave their families and their livelihood - and follow him. Only then would they inherit the Kingdom of God.

Anthony de Mello writes, "To find the kingdom is the easiest thing in the world but also the most difficult. Easy because it is all around you and within you, and all you have to

Christianity Without Beliefs

do is reach out and take possession of it. Difficult because if you wish to possess the kingdom you may possess nothing else."[19]

The earliest Christian movement was a community of religious mendicants who traveled the countryside proclaiming the Kingdom of God. Jesus told them, "Take nothing for your journey, no staff, nor bag, nor bread, nor money; and do not have two tunics." (Luke 9:3) Jesus' teaching on living a life of material simplicity is the longest section in the Sermon on the Mount:

> Do not lay up for yourselves treasures on earth, where moth and rust destroy and where thieves break in and steal, but lay up for yourselves treasures in heaven, where neither moth nor rust destroys and where thieves do not break in and steal. For where your treasure is, there your heart will be also.

> The eye is the lamp of the body. So, if your eye is healthy, your whole body will be full of light, but if your eye is bad, your whole body will be full of darkness. If then the light in you is darkness, how great is the darkness!

> No one can serve two masters, for either he will hate the one and love the other, or he will be devoted to the one and despise the other. You cannot serve God and money.

Therefore I tell you, do not be anxious about your life, what you will eat or what you will drink, nor about your body, what you will put on. Is not life more than food, and the body more than clothing? Look at the birds of the air: they neither sow nor reap nor gather into barns, and yet your heavenly Father feeds them. Are you not of more value than they? And which of you by being anxious can add a single hour to his span of life? And why are you anxious about clothing?

Consider the lilies of the field, how they grow: they neither toil nor spin, yet I tell you, even Solomon in all his glory was not arrayed like one of these. But if God so clothes the grass of the field, which today is alive and tomorrow is thrown into the oven, will he not much more clothe you, O you of little faith?

Therefore do not be anxious, saying, 'What shall we eat?' or 'What shall we drink?' or 'What shall we wear?' For the Gentiles seek after all these things, and your heavenly Father knows that you need them all. But seek first the kingdom of God and his righteousness, and all these things will be added to you.

Therefore do not be anxious about tomorrow, for tomorrow will be anxious for

Christianity Without Beliefs

itself. Sufficient for the day is its own trouble. (Matthew 6:19-34)

Jesus' words about the eye is the key to this passage: "The eye is the lamp of the body. So, if your eye is healthy, your whole body will be full of light, but if your eye is bad, your whole body will be full of darkness. If then the light in you is darkness, how great is the darkness!" How one views material things is the filter through which one sees God. If one's life is dominated by the desire for money and possessions, then one will see God and religion as a means to that end. In that case, how great is the darkness!

The American church is lost in darkness. Though Americans are among the richest people in the world, American Christians are anxious about financial security. They are blinded by the cultural obsession of consumerism. Megachurches have become temples to Mammon, their pastors more concerned about private jets than the poor. The only solution is to return to Jesus' gospel of simplicity. It is time to get out the whip of cords and clean house.

Tolerance

We live in age of intolerance, and it seems to be getting worse every year. The political rhetoric in the United States is the worst in my memory. Religion is dominated by extremes, and the moderate middle is disappearing. On the world stage the most dangerous forms of religion are fundamentalisms that advocate violence, suppression and persecution toward those who disagree with them on theological and ethical matters. This is true especially of Islamic, Hindu, and Christian forms of fundamentalism, but is found in other religions, including the normally nonviolent Buddhism, as evidenced in the genocide against Rohingya Muslims in Myanmar.

Intolerance is born from the conviction that "we" are right and "they" are wrong. The "other" is demonized as an inhuman evil that cannot be allowed to exist in society. "We" are on the side of God, and "they" are opposed to Godly values. It was illustrated a hundred years ago with the slogan "Gott mit Uns" (God with us) emblazoned on the belt buckles and helmets of German soldiers during the Great War.

It is echoed in the slogans of Christian evangelicals today who rewrite American history, refashioning the United States as a Christian nation, and calling for the dissolution of the "wall of separation" between church and state. The government endorsed mottos "In God we trust" on our currency and "one nation under God" in our pledge of allegiance make it clear that nonbelievers are not entirely welcome. Intolerance is finding expression most recently in the rise of racism, antisemitism, xenophobia and calls to secure our borders.

There will always be differences between people who hold strong beliefs – especially religious and moral beliefs. There seems to be no middle ground when it comes to divisive issues such as abortion and homosexuality. But the situation was no less divisive in Jesus' day, although the issues were different. Into such a poisonous religious and political environment Jesus spoke words advocating tolerance of those whom we believe are wrong.

Judge not, that you be not judged. For with the judgment you pronounce you will be judged, and with the measure you use it will be measured to you. Why do you see the speck that is in your brother's eye, but do not notice the log that is in your own eye? Or how can you say to your brother, 'Let me take the speck out of your eye,' when there is the log in your own eye? You hypocrite, first take the log out of your own eye, and then you will see clearly to take the speck out of your brother's eye. Do not give dogs what is holy, and do not throw your pearls before pigs, lest they trample them underfoot and turn to attack you. (Matthew 7:1-6)

This is not a call to abandon sincerely held beliefs and values. It is a call to consider the possibility that we might be wrong. This is a distinction that is lost in American culture. We tend to gravitate to one of two extremes – fundamentalism or relativism. Either we possess the absolute truth or there is no absolute truth. Either we are right (and everyone else is wrong), or it is all relative (and there is no right and wrong.) This extremism is not the exclusive domain of the religious or political right. The left can be just as self-righteous and blind to their own intolerance of opposing positions, as evidenced in "safe spaces" and speech codes on college campuses.

Into this atmosphere of polarization Jesus speaks a word calling us to step back and put ourselves in the other's shoes. This naturally leads to treating others as we would like to be treated, summed up in the Golden Rule, mentioned a couple of verses later. "So whatever you wish that others would do to you, do also to them, for this is the Law and the Prophets." (7:12)

Jesus says, "Judge not, that you be not judged." By judging others we are usurping the role of God. We are revealing to the world that we are so self-righteous that we are self-deceptive; we are blind and deaf to the possibility of our own sinfulness. To be judgmental is the height of hypocrisy and arrogance.

Jesus' words are a call to introspection. Like so often in the Sermon on the Mount, Jesus is reminding us that the spiritual life is inwardly directed. The way others live, what others believe, and what they say are not our concern – as long as they do no physical harm to others. We need to pay attention to the health of our own soul before we attempt to heal others' souls.

To forsake judging others does not mean that we have given up the responsibility to work for what is right and good in society. We can still discern right and wrong, good and evil. But we need to have the self-awareness to realize that we might not be as right as we think we are. There is still truth and falsehood, but we may not be the best judges of truth. It introduces an element of self-doubt into our assessment of ourselves and others.

In the small New Hampshire town in which I reside, we still govern ourselves by the centuries old democratic tradition of a town meeting. Every March, when the snow begins to melt and cabin fever begins to abate, the townspeople immerge from the warmth of their woodstoves and converge on the local school auditorium.

There we spend several hours arguing and voting on everything from the purchase of a new fire engine to the type of light bulbs to be used in the twenty streetlights that illumine the village center. Often feelings can run high and words are spoken in anger.

As it always has, the annual town meeting still begins with prayer, with the hope that a preemptive godly word might dampen the use of ungodly language. For years, as pastor of one of the two churches in town (the other being a Friends Meeting – which prefers communal silence to public prayer), I was the one who offered the invocation. At such times I was very aware that I was speaking not only for my Christian congregation but for my Jewish neighbors and the many nonbelievers in town, and I phrased my prayer accordingly.

One of the ministers in town, who would occasionally offer the invocation, was Leroy Rouner, author of the book "Civil Religion and Political Theology." Dr. Rouner was Professor of Philosophy, Religion, and Philosophical Theology and Director of the Institute for Philosophy and Religion at Boston University. The prayer that Lee Rouner offered in 2003 was so effective that it was voted to be read in perpetuity at the start of every town meeting. It is still being read today, more than a decade after his death. It reads in part: "Give us the courage of our convictions, but make us gentle with one another, respectful of views we do not share, mindful of the faint but humbling possibility that we may be wrong."[20]

This is the type of sentiment that Jesus was communicating. He was not advocating an abandonment of objective standards of truth or morality. But he was making it clear that his hearers were not the final arbiters of such absolutes. As Paul wrote in his famous Love Chapter, "For we know in part and we prophesy in part, but when the perfect comes, the partial will pass away. When I was a child, I spoke like a child, I thought like a child, I reasoned like a child. When I became a man, I gave up childish ways. For now we see in a mirror dimly, but then face to face. Now I know in part; then I shall know fully, even as I have been fully known." (I Corinthians 13:9-12) None of us have perfect knowledge, so we should temper our zeal, lest we find ourselves opposing God.

Individuality

The way of Christ is - to use Robert Frost's famous phrase - the road less traveled.

Two roads diverged in a wood, and I —
I took the one less traveled by,
And that has made all the difference.[21]

How many times have I heard these words quoted at High School Baccalaureate services? And how many times have I watched these teenagers proceed out of the doors to follow the herd into lives of conformity? Jesus was an individual. There was no one like him before or since. He was renowned for going his own way in religious matters. The Sermon on the Mount is filled with challenges to traditional religion. He would quote the Torah and then challenge it. "You have heard that it was said of old ... but I say to you..." What gall! To challenge the scriptures directly! No wonder he was executed!

When he finished his sermon the Gospel of Matthew says, "And when Jesus finished these sayings, the crowds were astonished at his teaching, for he was teaching them as one who had authority, and not as their scribes." (7:28-29) What nerve! To challenge the authority of the scribes! Everyone was opposed to Jesus – the teachers of the Law, the Pharisees, the Sadducees, the Herodians, the chief priests. Every religious group mentioned in the gospels was in opposition to the teachings of Jesus.

Jesus went his own way, and he calls us to follow his example. "Enter by the narrow gate. For the gate is wide and the way is easy that leads to destruction, and those who enter by it are many. For the gate is narrow and the way is hard that leads to life, and those who find it are few." (7:13-14)

We do not follow Jesus by mindlessly treading the well-beaten path of Christian orthodoxy. That is the wide gate and the broad way. To follow that way, there is no need to do any thinking. Just recite the creed. Do what the preacher says. Do not question authority. Absolutely do not question traditional interpretation of scripture. Never ... ever ... ever speak like Jesus: "You have heard that it was said to those of old... but I say to you..."

Christ was what they call a "maverick" these days. He was a spiritual pioneer. A true individual. A freethinker. A rebel. Today's Christians are not mavericks. The New Testament routinely use words like "sheep," "slaves" and "servants" to describe Christian believers. Instead of holding out arms wide in prayer to the inspiration of the Spirit (as the earliest artistic depictions of Christians in prayer), we fold our hands before us in the posture of slaves wearing shackles.

There is a Far Side cartoon by Gary Larson that shows a group of lemmings mindlessly running down a hill and over a cliff into the sea. But one lemming in the back of the herd has a sly smile on his face, and he is wearing a life preserver. Jesus encourages us to wear that smile. Be the maverick. Take the road less traveled. Go your own way. Blaze your own trail. Challenge the crowd. Question authority.

Swim against the current. It is easy to float with mainstream religion, but you will never develop any spiritual muscles. NPR journalist Shankar Vedantam says that those who travel with the current will always feel they are good swimmers, while those who swim against the current may never realize they are better swimmers than they imagine. You are a better swimmer than you imagine. But you will never know unless you try.

It is not easy to challenge the "powers that be" in any religion. It wasn't easy in Jesus' day, and it certainly isn't easy today. When we take the spiritual road less traveled, we will be warned it is too dangerous. We will threatened with excommunication and hell. We will be called names and persecuted. We will be labeled heretics and apostates. At such times we must remember the words of Jesus. "Blessed are you when others revile you and persecute you and utter all kinds of evil against you falsely on my account. Rejoice and be glad, for your reward is great in heaven, for so they persecuted the prophets who were before you." (5:11-12)

Discernment

Taking the "road less traveled" involves spiritual discernment. There are a lot of spiritual pitfalls out there. There are a lot of false teachers looking for disciples. Just because spiritual teachers are not part of "organized religion" or the "institutional church" does not mean that they are authentic voices of spiritual direction. Once we set out on our own and leave the relative safety of the flock, we have to be on the lookout for predators. Jesus says,

> Beware of false prophets, who come to you in sheep's clothing but inwardly are ravenous wolves. You will recognize them by their fruits. Are grapes gathered from thornbushes, or figs from thistles? So, every healthy tree bears good fruit, but the diseased tree bears bad fruit. A healthy tree cannot bear bad fruit, nor can a diseased tree bear good fruit. Every tree that does not bear good fruit is cut down and thrown into the fire. Thus you will recognize them by their fruits.

> "Not everyone who says to me, 'Lord, Lord,' will enter the kingdom of heaven, but the one who does the will of my Father

who is in heaven. On that day many will say to me, 'Lord, Lord, did we not prophesy in your name, and cast out demons in your name, and do many mighty works in your name?' And then will I declare to them, 'I never knew you; depart from me, you workers of lawlessness.' (Matthew 7:15-23)

The evangelical and mainline churches rightly warn us about the danger of "cults." There are a lot of religious charlatans out there on the spiritual teaching circuit. The danger of the deadness of mainline religion is nothing in comparison to the brainwashing and groupthink of splinter religious movements.

I am not just talking about quasi-Christian sects like Mormons and Jehovah's Witnesses, or offbeat groups like Scientology. Alternative spirituality and the New Age movement with their panoply of gurus and self-styled "spiritual teachers" are just as dangerous. Offers of spiritual enlightenment and awakening should be distrusted as much as offers of salvation from hell.

"There is a sucker born every minute," said P. T. Barnum, and nowhere is this more evident than in the subculture of American pop spirituality. Hucksters will sell you crystals that emit spiritual energy. They will balance your chakras, read your auras, or manipulate your spiritual energy with Reiki. They will channel long-dead "enlightened masters," recall your past lives, and teach you chants and mantras. They will weave intricate metaphysical systems that can keep you tangled in knots for a lifetime.

Jesus lumps all of these together under the name "false prophets." Christ calls us to discernment. He has one simple rule when it comes to these rogue teachers: "You will recognize them by their fruits." You will not know them by their teachings. Their teachings may sound good, but so did the words of the serpent in Eden. You cannot tell them by their "mighty works," especially those that appear miraculous or supernatural.

Jesus' sole standard for discernment is morality. "Depart from me, you workers of lawlessness." By this he means rejection of common moral standards. This can take various forms. Often it is present in the form of sexual misconduct by the one in spiritual authority. It also can take the form of deceit, emotional manipulation, or psychological abuse. One common form of immorality in spiritual circles is the love of money. False teachers have many clever strategies to separate spiritual seekers from their money.

A genuine spiritual teacher cannot love both God and Mammon. The request for money as part of a spiritual path is a sure sign that something is amiss. If a spiritual teacher expects money in exchange for spiritual instruction –

even if it is in the form of a "suggested donation," then walk away quickly. Be wary of initial come-ons that are free, only to result in a financial fleecing later down the road. The Way of Christ has no commerce with Mammon. The Kingdom of God is free. Jesus never took a shekel from anyone for his instruction.

The authentic spiritual life is an individual path of spiritual discernment that avoids both the highway of mass-produced religion and the byways of boutique spiritualties. The way of Jesus is blazed by hand in the wilderness. It is the way of the pioneer, the spiritual explorer and adventurer. Its guiding star is Christ. We are to "fix our eyes on Jesus, the pioneer and perfecter of faith." (Hebrews 12:2) As they say in the commercial, "accept no substitutes."

Decisiveness

Every sermon expects a response. Jesus' Sermon on the Mount is no exception. Attenders at tent revivals "walked the sawdust trail" to repent of their sins and accept Christ as Savior. "Mourners' benches" were placed in the front of Methodist churches to accommodate those who would come forward after the sermon seeking sanctification. Many Baptist churches still extend an "altar call" for people to be born again. Billy Graham made this practice famous with his invitation to people to walk to the front of the stadium while the choir sang "Just As I Am." John the Baptist invited his hearers to undergo a baptism of repentance for the forgiveness of sins. (Mark 1:4) Jesus expected a response from his hearers as well. He ended his sermon with these words:

> Everyone then who hears these words of mine and does them will be like a wise man who built his house on the rock. And the rain fell, and the floods came, and the winds blew and beat on that house, but it did not fall, because it had been founded on the rock. And everyone who hears these words of mine and does not do them will be like a foolish man who built his house on the sand. And

the rain fell, and the floods came, and the winds blew and beat against that house, and it fell, and great was the fall of it. (Matthew 7:24-27)

Jesus expected his followers not only to listen, but to act. People were not just to hear his words but to heed them. To act decisively. Decisiveness is an important quality of the spiritual life. Without decisiveness spirituality is no more than a leisure activity. It is a hobby or a pastime to do on weekends or holidays. All the qualities that Jesus mentions in the Sermon on the Mount are useless if they are not incarnated in our lives daily. That takes a decision to act.

Decisiveness is the ability to recognize the importance of the call to the spiritual life and to respond accordingly. It places the spiritual life above all other responsibilities. Jesus instructed a man to follow him. The man replied, "Lord, let me first go and bury my father." Jesus said to him, "Leave the dead to bury their own dead. But as for you, go and proclaim the kingdom of God." Yet another said, "I will follow you, Lord, but let me first say farewell to those at my home." Jesus said to him, "No one who puts his hand to the plow and looks back is fit for the kingdom of God." (Luke 9:59-62) Jesus did not tolerate indecision.

Too much of modern spirituality is half-hearted. Church services and spiritual teachings are designed to do little more than titillate the spiritual curiosity of the hearer. Too much of evangelical worship is entertainment.[22] Not much is expected of the hearer except to have a good time and keep coming back – and of course contribute your money. At most, people receive interesting insights in the form of self-help maxims that can be added to one's collection of spiritual ideas and applied to daily life.

Jesus expected much more than that. He wanted his followers to build their lives on the truths in this sermon. He likened his teachings to a house that would be lived in, not just a building to be visited occasionally. His teaching is a house strong enough to withstand the storms of life. He ought to know. He was a carpenter. Here he plies his trade to construct a spiritual house that can survive floods and hurricanes. The Sermon on the Mount is more than a pleasant Sunday morning homily. It is a prophetic call to action. It is a call to commit oneself to the spiritual life without reservation.

Christianity Beyond Beliefs

Imagine there's no heaven
It's easy if you try
No hell below us
Above us only sky
Imagine all the people
Living for today... Aha-ah...[23]

Imagine Christianity without beliefs. Without heaven or hell, without the Virgin Birth or the Second Coming, without the Trinity or the Incarnation. It is not easy for today's Christians to imagine such a thing. We are indoctrinated (literally) to the idea that Christianity is a collection of beliefs. It is drilled into us that if we do not accept these doctrines – or at least a few of the basic ones – then we are not really Christians.

But we have seen in this book that this is not true. All these theological concepts are late developments in the history of the Christian faith. But aren't these doctrines true? Yes, they are true. But they are theologically true, not literally true. They are metaphorically true, not metaphysically true. They are symbolically true, not scientifically true. They are mythically true, not historically true. Doctrines are meant to point to truth. They must not to be mistaken for truths.

Beliefs are not essential to Christianity. There was a time before Christianity was a doctrinal religion. There was a time before Christianity was a religion at all. There was a time before it had Scriptures and creeds and clergy. There was a time when the teachings of Jesus were just a way of living. It was simply called "the Way" by the early followers of Jesus." (Acts 9:2; 19:9, 23; 22:4) There was a time when the teachings of Jesus described a spiritual path, not a religious system of beliefs and rituals. It can be that way again.

No Creed but Christ

The earliest creedal statement in the New Testament is the simple phrase "Jesus is Lord." In Greek it consists of only two words: κύριος Ἰησοῦς or kyrios Iesous. It is quoted repeatedly by the Apostle Paul in his epistles, which are the earliest writings of the New Testament (1 Corinthians 12:3; Romans 10:9; Philippians 2:11). It was probably the confession of faith used at the earliest baptisms (Acts 8:16; 19:5; 1 Corinthians 6:11). To say those words identified one as a Christian.

Christians of all varieties in the earliest decades of the Christian movement united behind this simple declaration of faith, regardless of how they differed in other matters. It is what unified churches with various understandings of the nature and mission of Jesus of Nazareth. It is for this reason that the phrase "Jesus is Lord" is the motto of the World Council of Churches today.

Islam has a simple requirement for being a Muslim. All one has to do is recite the Shahada, which simply means "the testimony." It is: "There is no God but God, and Muhammad is his prophet." That is it! Christianity could learn something from Islam. The only requirement for being a Christian should be to say the words "Jesus is Lord." As the apostle Paul wrote, "No one can say 'Jesus is Lord' except in the Holy Spirit." (I Corinthians 12:3) This would be the Christian testimony, a Christian Shahada.

No Law but Love

Along with the simple creed "Jesus is Lord" there is an equally simple Christian ethic: Love. This was Jesus' summary of the Hebrew Scriptures. "You shall love the Lord your God with all your heart and with all your soul and with all your mind. This is the great and first commandment. And a second is like it: You shall love your neighbor as yourself. On these two commandments depend all the Law and the Prophets." (Matthew 22:38-40)

In the Gospel of John, Jesus sums up all the commandments of God in one "new commandment." "A new commandment I give to you, that you love one another: just as I have loved you, you also are to love one another. By this all people will know that you are my disciples, if you have love for one another." (John 13:34-35; see also 15:12)

The First Epistle of John identifies love as the defining characteristic of the Christian and goes so far as to say that "God is Love." He writes, "Beloved, let us love one another, for love is from God, and whoever loves has been born of God and knows God. Anyone who does not love does not know God, because God is love." (I John 4:7-8) As another John Lennon song says, "All You Need Is Love." As I earlier quoted Augustine as saying, "Love, and do what you will."

Psychiatrist Viktor Frankl came to this conclusion after experiencing firsthand the horrors of a Nazi concentration camp. He wrote in his famous book, *Man's Search for Meaning*: "A thought transfixed me: for the first time in my life I saw the truth as it is set into song by so many poets, proclaimed as the final wisdom by so many thinkers. The truth — that love is the ultimate and the highest goal to which man can aspire. Then I grasped the meaning of the greatest secret that human poetry and human thought and belief have to impart: The salvation of man is through love and in love."[24]

These two simple statements "Jesus is Lord" and "Love one another" are a good summary of the spiritual path of Jesus. Many readers will think this approach is simplistic and idealistic. It undoubtedly is. I am under no illusion that the religionists of the world – the fundamentalists and traditionalists of Christianity – will abandon their beliefs and adopt these two simple principles. Nor am I under any illusion that the Sermon on the Mount will be taken seriously by Christians. His sermon has not been heeded by the church for two thousand years, and I don't see that changing anytime soon. But I can dream, can't I?

You may say I'm a dreamer
But I'm not the only one
I hope someday you'll join us
And the world will live as one.[25]

About the Author

Marshall Davis is an ordained American Baptist minister who has served churches in New Hampshire, Massachusetts, Pennsylvania, Illinois and Kentucky during his forty year ministry as a pastor.

He holds a Bachelor of Arts degree in Religion from Denison University, as well Master of Divinity and Doctor of Ministry degrees from the Southern Baptist Theological Seminary, Louisville, Kentucky. He is the author of seventeen books (and counting).

Having retired from fulltime pastoral ministry, nowadays he spends most days at his 18th century home in a small New Hampshire village in the White Mountains. He writes nearly every day, preaches occasionally, and plays with grandchildren often.

Find out more at amazon.com/Marshall-Davis/e/B001K8Y0RU/

Or visit revmdavis.blogspot.com/

OTHER BOOKS BY MARSHALL DAVIS

What Your Pastor Won't Tell You (But I Can Because I'm Retired)

Understanding Revelation

The Evolution of Easter: How the Historical Jesus Became the Risen Christ

The Seeker's Journey: A Contemporary Retelling of Pilgrim's Progress

The Parables of Jesus: American Paraphrase Version

Thank God for Atheists: What Christians Can Learn from the New Atheism

Experiencing God Directly: The Way of Christian Nonduality

The Tao of Christ: A Christian Version of the Tao Te Ching

Living Presence: A Guide to Everyday Awareness of God

More Than a Purpose: An Evangelical Response to Rick Warren and the Megachurch Movement

The Baptist Church Covenant: Its History and
Meaning

A People Called Baptist: An Introduction to
Baptist History & Heritage

The Practice of the Presence of God in Modern
English by Brother Lawrence, translated by
Marshall Davis

The Gospel of Solomon: The Christian Message
in the Song of Solomon

Esther

The Hidden Ones

Endnotes

[1] I got this phrase from Matthew Fox's book *Original Blessing.*

[2] Jesse Bering, "Never Say Die: Why We Can't Imagine Death," Scientific American Mind Magazine, Volume 19, Issue 5, October 2008, https://www.scientificamerican.com/article/never-say-die/

[3] Sigmund Freud, Reflections on War and Death, 1918. https://www.bartleby.com/282/2.html

[4] Quoted in the blog *Saganist*, "Why we can't imagine death" Nov, 16, 2008. http://saganist.blogspot.com/2008/11/why-we-cant-imagine-death.html

[5] All three of these excerpts are from my translation of the Chinese classic. Marshall Davis, *The Tao of Christ: A Christian Version of the Tao Te Ching* (Chapter 78). Kindle Edition.

[6] Steven Novella, Bob Novella, Cara Santa Maria, Jay Novella, Evan Bernstein, "The Skeptics' Guide to the Universe: How to Know What's Really Real in a World Increasingly Full of Fake" Grand Central Publishing. Kindle Edition, pp. 9-10,

[7] This is from my translation, The Parables of Jesus, *American Paraphrase Version, location 450*

[8] "The Top 25 Most Influential Preachers". Christianity Today. 2006. https://web.archive.org/web/20060201142833/http://www.christianitytoday.com/anniversary/features/top25preachers.html

[9] Social Injustice and the Gospel by John MacArthur, https://www.gty.org/library/blog/B180813

[10] Introduction of The Statement on Social Justice & the Gospel, https://statementonsocialjustice.com/#introduction

[11] Evelyn Underhill, *Mysticism: A Study of the Nature and Development of Man's Spiritual Consciousness*, 1911. Twelfth edition published by E. P. Dutton in 1930. Republished by Dover Publications in 2002.

[12] The Tao of Christ: A Christian Version of the Tao Te Ching, Marshall Davis, (p. 15). Kindle Edition.

[13] "Coptic Christians Receive Nobel Peace Prize Nomination," PRNewswire, https://www.prnewswire.com/news-releases/coptic-christians-receive-nobel-peace-prize-nomination-300717756.html

[14] Eknath Easwaran, The Chandogya Upanishad, 13:1-3, The

Upanishads (Classic of Indian Spirituality) (pp. 136-137). Nilgiri Press. Kindle Edition.

[15] Bonhoeffer, Dietrich, *Dietrich Bonhoeffer Works, vol. 8: Letters and Papers from Prison*, Fortress Press, 2010.

[16] Augustine, Seventh Homily on the First Epistle of John, 1 John 4:4-12, paragraph 8, translated by H. Browne. From Nicene and Post-Nicene Fathers, First Series, Vol. 7. Edited by Philip Schaff. (Buffalo, NY: Christian Literature Publishing Co., 1888.) http://www.newadvent.org/fathers/170207.htm

[17] "Bandwidth (An Analog Novel Book 1)" by Eliot Peper, p. 37.

[18] "Prosperity Gospel Taught to 4 in 10 Evangelical Churchgoers" Bob Smietana, Christianity Today, JULY 31, 2018, https://www.christianitytoday.com/news/2018/july/prosperity-gospel-survey-churchgoers-prosper-tithe-blessing.html

[19] The Way to Love : The Last Meditations of Anthony de Mello (1995)

[20] "Prayer for Town Meeting 2003" taken from the notes of Sandwich NH town moderator Lee Quimby.

[21] Robert Frost, "The Road Not Taken" 1916

[22] I explore this topic at length in a chapter entitled "Gimme That Showtime Religion" in my book *More Than a Purpose: An Evangelical Response to Rick Warren and the Megachurch Movement,* Chapter 4, Pleasant Word, 2006.

[23] "Imagine" written by Written by John Lennon &, Yoko Ono Release Date October 11, 1971.

[24] Viktor Frankl, *Man's Search for Meaning,* Beacon: Boston, 1946, p. 37.

[25] "Imagine" written by Written by John Lennon &, Yoko Ono Release Date October 11, 1971

Made in the USA
Middletown, DE
18 September 2020

19968237R00078